RVer's Guide to DUMP STATIONS

A comprehensive directory of
RV dump stations across the United States

Published by
Roundabout Publications
PO Box 19235
Lenexa, KS 66285

Phone
800-455-2207

Internet
www.RoundaboutPublications.com

Published by Roundabout Publications, PO Box 19235, Lenexa, KS 66285 / 800-455-2207

ISBN-10: 1-885464-39-8
ISBN-13: 978-1-885464-39-2

CONTENTS

INTRODUCTION

This book is designed to help you easily locate RV dump stations across America. Understanding how to use it will aid you in your search.

Dump station locations are organized by state. Those easily accessed from Interstate highways are listed first, followed by those in other locations. Interstate highways are listed by their number from lowest to highest. For dump stations in other locations, each site is listed alphabetically by city or town name.

Interstate Highways
RV dump stations located along Interstate highways are presented in a chart. Depending on your direction of travel, you'll either read up the chart or down the chart (see **Understanding Mile Markers and Exit Numbers** below). If you are traveling north or east, read up the chart. If you are traveling south or west, read down the chart.

Exit numbers are listed in bold type. The column next to the exit number shows the city, town, street, or other highways accessed from that exit. Beneath the exit name is a list of each site that has a dump station. Included are truck stops and travel centers, gas stations, city and county parks, and other sites.

Any location, such as a rest area or welcome center, that is located *along* an Interstate (not at an exit) is identified by its mile marker number surrounded by parentheses. Sometimes you will notice an (nb), (sb), (eb), or (wb) after the site name. This means that the facility is only accessible to northbound, southbound, eastbound, or westbound travelers.

Other Locations
Dump stations not located along Interstate highways are listed in this section. Each site is listed alphabetically by city or town name.

Understanding Mile Markers and Exit Numbers

Mile markers, or mileposts as they are also known, are the vertical green signs on the edge of highways placed at one-mile intervals. Mile marker numbering begins at the most southerly or westerly point in a state. For example, if you enter Colorado from New Mexico, mile markers will increase as you travel north through Colorado. Likewise if you were to enter Colorado from Utah, mile markers would increase as you travel east through Colorado. California is the only state that does not use mile markers. Instead they use a Post Mile system with numbering beginning and ending at county lines.

Interstate exit numbers are determined by one of two methods. The first, and most widely used, is based on the mile marker system. Using this method, the first exit number on an Interstate as you travel south to north or west to east is determined by its distance from the state line. For example, if an exit is located between mile markers 4 and 5, it is numbered as Exit 4. The next exit, if located at mile marker 8.7, would be numbered as Exit 8. Thus you would know that you must travel approximately 4 miles to reach the next exit. Using this method of exit numbering helps to determine the location and distance to a desired exit.

The second method of numbering Interstate exits is the consecutive numbering system, which means Interstate exit numbers begin at the most southerly or westerly point and increase consecutively as you travel north or east. Using this method, the first exit on an Interstate as you travel south to north or west to east is Exit 1. Each exit thereafter increases consecutively as Exit 2, Exit 3 and so on. Few states use this method.

As mentioned above, California does not use mile markers nor does it indicate exits with a number. This is changing, however. In January of 2002, California began erecting signs displaying exit numbers based on the mile marker system. The exit numbers and mile marker numbers used in this book are based on the proposed numbers that California has assigned.

Abbreviations

Below is a list of abbreviations used in this book.

Abbreviation	Description
Blvd	Boulevard
CR	County Road
E	East
eb	Eastbound
FM	Farm to Market Road
Hwy	Highway
I	Interstate
N	North
nb	Northbound
NRA	National Recreation Area
Pkwy	Parkway
Rd	Road
S	South
sb	Southbound
US	U.S. Highway
W	West
wb	Westbound

Final Note

Please keep in mind that public dump stations are subject to closure for a number of reasons including state budget cuts and dump station abuse. See Appendix C for more information about dump station abuse.

ALABAMA

Below is a list of RV dump stations in Alabama. Listed first are those easily accessed from Interstate highways followed by those in other locations throughout the state.

Interstate 10

Interstate 10 runs east to west for 67 miles from the Florida state line to the Mississippi state line. Eastbound travelers should read up the chart. Westbound travelers read down the chart.

Exit(mm)	Description
53	**CR 64 / Robertsdale** Oasis Travel Center, 27801 County Road 64, Robertsdale AL 36567 / 251-960-1148. Fee unknown.
44	**AL 59 / Loxley** Econ Family Travel Center, 14902 N Hickory St, Loxley AL 36551 / 251-964-5590 Love's Travel Stop, 126 E Flying K Rd, Loxley AL 36551 / 251-964-2090. Free. Latitude: 30.6520 • Longitude: -87.7568
22	**AL 163 / Dauphin Island Pkwy / Mobile** Shady Acres Campground, 2500 Old Military Rd, Mobile AL 36605 / 251-478-0013. Free. Latitude: 30.6275 • Longitude: -88.0956 *Comments*: From exit go south on AL 163 to first light, turn right on Old Military Rd, one block on the right, potable water available. Westbound travelers should use Exit 22b.
(1)	**Grand Bay Welcome Center (eb)** Restrooms, Phones, Picnic Tables, Vending Machines, RV Dump Station, Pet Walk Area, Handicap Facilities, Security. Latitude: 30.4776 • Longitude: -88.3893

Interstate 20

Interstate 20 runs east to west for approximately 215 miles from the Georgia state line to the Mississippi state line. A portion of the highway from Birmingham to Mississippi is also I-59. Eastbound travelers should read up the chart. Westbound travelers read down the chart.

Exit(mm)	Description
(213)	Welcome Center (wb)
▼ *I-20 and I-59 run together* ▼	
104	**McAshan Dr / Rock Mountain Lake**
	Flying J Travel Plaza
(85)	Rest Area
77	**Buttermilk Rd / to Cottondale**
	TA Travel Center
(39)	Rest Area (wb)
(38)	Rest Area (eb)
(.5)	Welcome Center (eb)
▲ *I-20 and I-59 run together* ▲	

Interstate 59

Interstate 59 runs north to south for 242 miles from the Georgia state line to the Mississippi state line. A portion of the highway from Birmingham to Mississippi is also I-20. Northbound travelers should read up the chart. Southbound travelers read down the chart.

Exit(mm)	Description
(241)	Welcome Center (sb)
(168)	Rest Area (sb)
(165)	Rest Area (nb)
▼ *I-20 and I-59 run together* ▼	
104	**McAshan Dr / Rock Mountain Lake**
	Flying J Travel Plaza
(85)	Rest Area
77	**Buttermilk Rd / to Cottondale**
	TA Travel Center
(39)	Rest Area (sb)
(38)	Rest Area (nb)
(.5)	Welcome Center (nb)
▲ *I-20 and I-59 run together* ▲	

Interstate 65

Interstate 65 runs north to south for 367 miles from the Tennessee state line to Interstate 10. Northbound travelers should read up the chart. Southbound travelers read down the chart.

Exit(mm)	Description
(364)	Welcome Center (sb)
334	**AL 67 / Priceville / to Decatur**
	Pilot Travel Center
(302)	Rest Area
264	**41st Ave / Daniel Payne Dr / Birmingham**
	Flying J Travel Plaza, 224 Daniel Payne Dr N, 205-323-2177, free.
	Latitude: 33.5622 • Longitude: -86.8305
(213)	Rest Area
158	**CR 6 / Tyson Rd / to Hayneville**
	Flying J Travel Plaza, 900 Tyson Rd, 334-613-0212, free. Latitude:
	32.1944 • Longitude: -86.4194
(134)	Rest Area
(89)	Rest Area (sb)
(85)	Welcome Center (nb)
19	**US 43 / to Satsuma**
	Pilot Travel Center

Interstate 85

Interstate 85 runs north to south for 80 miles from the Georgia state line to I-65 in Montgomery. Northbound travelers should read up the chart. Southbound travelers read down the chart.

Exit(mm)	Description
(78)	Welcome Center (sb)
(44)	Rest Area

Other Locations

City or Town	Description
Centre	Amoco on US 411
Dothan	Flying J Travel Plaza, 2190 Ross Clark Cir, Dothan AL 36301 / 334-792-5152. Free. The store is located south of town on the northeast corner of Ross Clark Cir and US-231. Latitude: 31.1905 • Longitude: -85.4005
Dothan	Welcome Center on US 231 at Alabama/Florida state line, 12 miles south of Dothan, no charge
Eufaula	Rest area on US 431 about 5 miles south of town. Free.
Marion	Lakeview Park near the public golf course, $10
Florala	Rest area on US 331 about 10 miles north of Florala. Attendants keep this clean. Free.
Maplesville	Rest area on north side of US 82, 3/4 mile west of AL Hwy 22, Free
Ozark	Inland Travel Stop on US 231 at AL 123. Easy access north or south bound. Dump site is on the west side of the building. Free
Ozark	Rest area on southbound side of US-231 at mile marker 38 about 5 miles south of town. 24-hour attendant, water hose at dump site. Free
Troy	Deer Run RV Park on US 231 north of town, 1-800-552-3036 or 334-566-6517, $10
Wetumpka	Fort Toulouse/Jackson Park campground west of US 231 on Fort Toulouse Rd
Woodville	Parnell Creek RV Park, 24 miles east of Huntsville off US 72 at Parnell Cir, $5 fee

ALASKA

Below is a list of RV dump stations in Alaska.

Other Locations

City or Town	Description
Anchorage	Holiday gas station, 1501 Abbott Rd, east side of Seward Hwy at Dimond Exit. Free
Anchorage	Holiday gas station on Old Seward Hwy, north of O'Malley Rd, no fee
Anchorage	Holiday gas station, 285 Muldoon Rd, 907-333-5222, fee unknown. Dump station is next to the propane tanks behind the store. Gas station is about 1/4 mile south of the Glenn Hwy.
Anchorage	Holiday gas station, 717 E Northern Lights Blvd, 907-272-8730. Located just west of Seward Hwy (AK 1) at Northern Lights Blvd. Dump station is on the west side of the building. Free
Anchorage	Tesoro gas station at Northern Lights Blvd and "A" St, just east of the retail building on a side street; look for the propane tanks, no fee
Dead Horse	NANA Oilfield Services Inc at end of Dalton Highway, go west 2.2 miles to the Time and Temp sign.
Eagle	Eagle Trading Company on Taylor Hwy at mile marker 161
Eagle River	Holiday gas station, 12021 Glenn Hwy, 907-694-1229, no charge. Dump is behind station on gravel area. Coming from the east, take the first Eagle River exit; cross highway and turn right at light. Gas station is on left several blocks down. Latitude: 61.3302 • Longitude: -149.5672
Eagle River	Tesoro gas station, 12139 Old Glenn Hwy, 907-696-3120, no charge. Dump is in back, access from east side of station by car wash for from side street west of station. Potable water also available. Coming from the east, take the first Eagle River exit; cross highway and turn right at light. Gas station is on left several blocks down. Latitude: 61.3316 • Longitude: -149.5659
Fairbanks	Alaska Chevron, 333 Illinois St, 907-452-3025, fee unknown
Fairbanks	Chena River State Recreation Site (also known as Chena River Wayside), 221 University Ave, $5 or free if camping.

Fairbanks	Holiday gas station at 23rd and Cushman streets
Fairbanks	Mike's University Chevron, 3245 College Rd, 907-479-7060, fee unknown
Fairbanks	Sourdough Fuel on Johansen Expy at Danby, no water, large area to get in and out, free
Fairbanks	Tanana Valley State Fairgrounds along College Rd, fee unknown
Fairbanks	Tesoro Truck Stop at Cushman and Van Horn streets
Haines	Bigfoot Auto Service at 987 Haines Hwy
Haines	Delta Western gas station at 900 W Main St
Homer	Public dump station directly across Sterling Highway from the large US Post Office located at 3658 Heath St. Dump site is at the southeast corner of Sterling Highway and Heath St. Fresh water available.
Juneau	Mendenhall Lake Campground (US Forest Service) about 13 miles northwest of Juneau off AK 7
Ketchikan	Ketchikan Public Works at 3291 Tongass Ave, 2 blocks north of ferry terminal, no charge
Kodiak	Petro Express, 2597 Mill Bay Rd, Kodiak AK 99615 / 907-486-6511. Free. Located on the left side of the building by the car wash. Latitude: 57.8085 • Longitude: -152.3664
North Pole	Chena Lake Recreation Area, 907-488-1655, located three miles off Richardson Hwy on Laurance Rd.
North Pole	Santaland RV Park, 125 St Nicholas Dr, 907-488-9123 or 888-488-9123, Fee unknown
Palmer	Chevron gas station at intersection of Glenn Hwy and Palmer-Wasilla Rd, $2 or free with fuel purchase.
Soldotna	Fred Meyer, 43843 Sterling Hwy. Parking lot striped for RVs on north side. Overnighters welcome.
Tok	Tesoro Northern Energy Corp on Alaska Hwy at mile marker 1314
Tok	Young's Chevron at Alaska Hwy and Glenn Hwy
Valdez	Tesoro at Meals Ave and Eagen Ave
Wasilla	Chevron gas station on Parks Hwy next to Wells Fargo Bank, east end of town, $5 or free with fuel purchase.
Wasilla	This Holiday Gas Station is the last station heading north to Fairbanks on the Parks Highway. The dump and propane is in the back of the building. There is no fee.

Arizona

Below is a list of RV dump stations in Arizona. Listed first are those easily accessed from Interstate highways followed by those in other locations throughout the state.

Interstate 8

Interstate 8 runs east to west for about 178 miles from Interstate 10 to the California state line. Eastbound travelers should read up the chart. Westbound travelers read down the chart.

Exit(mm)	Description
119	**Butterfield Trail / to Gila Bend** Holt's Shell Truck Stop & RV Park, 3006 Butterfield Trail, Gila Bend AZ 85337 / 928-683-2449. Free. Dump station in rear of gas station near old white box railcar. Location also has free water, air, and wireless Internet. Large lot with RV park in rear of property. Latitude: 32.9307 • Longitude: -112.6737
115	**AZ 85 / to Gila Bend** Love's Travel Stop, 820 W Pima St, Gila Bend AZ 85337 / 928-683-2210. Free. Latitude: 32.9439 • Longitude: -112.7329
30	**William St / Wellton** Chevron Station, 28864 Commerce Way, Welton AZ 85356. Free. La Paz RV Park, 10319 Maybelle St, 928-785-4987, $5. From exit, go north to Los Angeles Ave and go west three blocks to Maybelle St. RV park is on the north side of road.
3	**S Avenue 3E / Yuma** Love's Travel Stop, 2931 E Gila Ridge Rd, Yuma AZ 85365 / 928-341-9100. Cost is $7. Dump station is in front of car fuel island.

Interstate 10

Interstate 10 runs east to west for about 391 miles from the New Mexico state line to the California state line. Eastbound travelers should read up the chart. Westbound travelers read down the chart.

Exit(mm)	Description
340	**AZ 186 / to Willcox** TA Travel Center, 1501 Fort Grant Rd, 520-384-5311, free. Pull-thru access on RV fuel island with potable water, adjacent to propane.

302	**AZ 90 S**
	Gas City Truck Stop
275	**Houghton Rd / southeast of Tucson**
	Pima County Fairgrounds, 11300 S Houghton Rd, Tucson AZ 85747 / 520-762-9100. $5 Latitude: 32.0486 • Longitude: -110.7823
270	**S Kolb Rd / south of Tucson**
	Gas City at E Valencia Rd and S Kolb Rd, about two miles north of exit. Free
268	**Craycroft Rd / Tucson**
	Triple T Truck Stop, 5451 Benson Hwy, Tucson AZ 85706 / 520-574-0050. Free. Water available. Latitude: 32.1267 • Longitude: -110.8766
264	**Irvington Rd / Tucson**
	Camping World / Beaudry RV Park; west on Irvington Rd; Beaudry's RV Park is on left. Take a left at the "T" in the road and on the right in cul-de-sac is dump station and fresh water. Free
254	**Prince Rd**
	Arizona Roadrunner RV Service Center, 4324 N Flowing Wells Rd, free
	Comments: From exit travel east to third traffic light, turn left (north) on Flowing Wells Rd and go north about one mile.
208	**Sunshine Blvd / to Eloy**
	Flying J Travel Plaza
	Pilot Travel Center
203	**Toltec Rd / to Eloy**
	TA Travel Center
137	**N 67th Ave / Phoenix**
	Flying J Travel Plaza, 6700 W Latham, 623-936-1118, Free. Latitude: 33.4613 • Longitude: -112.2222
94	**411th Ave / Tonopah**
	El Dorado Hot Springs, 41225 Indian School Rd
	Comments: Dump is free with purchase of a hot mineral water soak, located 1/4 mile west of 411th Ave
45	**Vicksburg Rd**
	Tomahawk Auto & Truck Plaza, $5 fee
19	**I-10 Bus / Quartzsite**
	RV Pit Stop, 425 N Central Blvd, 928-927-3714, $7. Propane and fresh water also available ($3 fee for water fill up). Latitude: 33.6720 • Longitude: -114.2168

Interstate 17

Interstate 17 runs north to south for about 147 miles from I-40 in Flagstaff to I-10 in Phoenix. Northbound travelers should read up the chart. Southbound travelers read down the chart.

Exit(mm)	Description
322	**Pinewood Rd / Munds Park** Munds Park RV Resort, 17550 Munds Ranch Rd, 928-286-1309 or 800-243-1309, $10. Latitude: 34.9424 • Longitude: -111.6565
287	**AZ 260 / Finnie Flats Rd / Camp Verde** Shell gas station just off the Interstate next to McDonald's, $5 fee
205	**W Glendale Ave / Phoenix** Gas station on N 35th Ave, one mile west of exit, $10 fee

Interstate 40

Interstate 40 runs east to west for 360 miles from the New Mexico state line to the California state line. Eastbound travelers should read up the chart. Westbound travelers read down the chart.

Exit(mm)	Description
255	**to I-40 Bus / Winslow** Flying J Travel Plaza
198	**Butler Ave / to Flagstaff** Conoco at 2300 E Butler (free)
123	**I-40-BUS / Seligman** KOA, 801 E Highway 66, Seligman AZ 86337 / 928-422-3358. Cost is $8. Latitude: 35.3227 • Longitude: -112.8560
59	**CR 259 / DW Ranch Rd** Love's Travel Stop
53	**AZ 66 / Andy Devine Ave / to Kingman** Flying J Travel Plaza

Other Locations

City or Town	Description
Bouse	Bouse Community Park (county park) on Plomosa Rd west of AZ Hwy 72, 928-667-2069, $5 if camping, $10 if not. Water available (included in fee).

Cave Creek	Superpumper, 4740 E Dynamite Blvd, 480-419-9037, free. Store is about 5 miles north of AZ 101 Exit 31. Latitude: 33.7410 • Longitude: -111.9787
Chandler	Public dump station at the car wash on E Riggs Rd, just east of S McQueen Rd, on north side of road, $5. Car wash is about five miles east of I-10 Exit 167.
Chinle	Free campground and dump station at the Visitors Center at Canyon de Chelly National Monument. Water at dump site is turned off in winter but there is a fresh water tap on the grounds.
Cottonwood	Giant Service Station, 999 S Main St, Cottonwood AZ 86326 / 928-634-8459. Free. Air and water also available.
Cottonwood	Verde Valley Fairgrounds at S 12th St and Hwy 89A
Flagstaff	Giant Service Station at 1205 S Milton (free)
Fountain Hills	McDowell Mountain Park (county park), 480-471-0173, free if camping. Individuals who are not camping in the park will be charged the camping fee to use the dump station. From Shea Blvd follow Fountain Hills Blvd north through town and then four miles north. Open year-round. Can handle two units at one time. Usually not crowded and has potable water available.
Gila Bend	Minute Mart at 942 E AZ 85
Gilbert	Shell Mini-Mart Car Wash on the corner of Ray Rd and Lindsay, next to the Osco drug store, $12
Heber	Public dump station near Woods Canyon Lake in Sitgreaves National Forest, $6. The dump station is about 25 miles west of town and four miles north of AZ 260 via FSR 300 and FSR 105.
Laveen	Laveen Mini Storage, 4410 W Southern Ave, Laveen AZ 85339 / 602-237-1803. Cost is unknown. Latitude: 33.3920 • Longitude: -112.1532
Mesa	Apache Sands Car Care Center (U-Haul) at 7602 E Apache Trail, $8 fee
Mesa	Chevron Station, 1143 N Ellsworth Rd, Mesa AZ 85207 / 480-357-3822. Cost is $5.
Mesa	Desert RV Parts & Service Center at 9736 E Apache Trail, $4-5 fee
Morenci	Conoco Gas/Convenience store just off US 191, free, watch for sign, water available
Oro Valley	Giant Gas Station, 10505 N Oracle Rd, 520-742-3275, no charge, water available. Latitude: 32.3959 • Longitude: -110.9601

Page	Shell Service Station, 901 N US-89, Page AZ 86040 / 928-645-5998. Cost is unknown. Located at the junction of US-89 and Haul Rd, across the street from the new Wal-Mart Supercenter. This is north of the junction of US-89 and SH-98. Has dump, water, air, propane, gas, diesel. Has 2 large RV/Truck lanes for fuel in the back of the station. Nice and easy to get in and out of this station. Latitude: 36.9046 • Longitude: -111.4841
Payson	Giant Gas Station, 701 E Highway 260, Payson AZ 85541 / 928-474-5200. Free. There are two dump stations located on the west side of the parking lot.
Payson	Happy Jack Lodge & RV Resort, 928-477-2805, $5. North of Clints Well on Lake Mary Rd and about 40 miles north of Payson via AZ 87. Drinking water for 10 cents per gallon available.
Payson	Houston Mesa Campground (928-474-7658) in Tonto National Forest north of town, just east of AZ 87
Phoenix	Bell Road RV Center, 2727 E Bell Rd, 602-971-2450, $2, open Mon-Sat
Pine	Uncle Tom's Kwik Stop, 4101 N Hwy 87, Pine AZ 85544 / 928-476-4105. Fee unknown.
Prescott	Affinity RV, 3197 Willow Creek Rd, 928-445-7910, free. Their One-Stop Traveler's Oasis offers the following free services: evacuate and flush holding tanks; check tires (including spare); inspect tow vehicle; wash all windows, mirrors and headlights (including tow vehicle); and fill fresh water tank. Latitude: 34.5951 • Longitude: -112.4662
Prescott	City wastewater treatment plant on Sundog Ranch Rd off AZ 89 about two miles north of town, open 7 days a week, closes earlier on weekends and holidays, no charge
Prescott Valley	Many Trails RV, 6850 E Hwy 69, Prescott Valley AZ 86314 / 928-775-5770 or 800-479-5770. Free.
Roosevelt	Cholla Bay Recreation Site (national forest campground) on AZ 188 at milepost 249, north of Roosevelt, no charge
Safford	The city of Safford provides a free dump station but no drinking water at the city waste disposal plant located on N 8th Ave near the Gila River. The site is designed for septic tanker trucks with outlets at the rear of the truck, so the reach is a little long for RV's with side outlets.
Safford	Champion Home Center, 711 E US-70, Safford AZ 85546 / 866-835-4437 or 928-428-4437. Cost is unknown. Dump station and water located next to the two elm trees at the

	entrance. Enter off 8th St as the US-70 entrance might be a little steep for some RVs.
Scottsdale	Public dump station in WestWorld equestrian center. From AZ 101 Loop, take the Frank Lloyd Wright Blvd exit and follow signs. $3 fee. Pay at RV office before dumping.
Scottsdale	Shell gas station at 4001 N Pima Rd, 480-947-6400, $10 fee. Located off the Hwy 101 Loop at Indian School Rd, west of exit. Latitude: 33.4934 • Longitude: -111.8916
Sierra Vista	Gas City near junction of AZ 90 and AZ 92 next to Ford dealership. Free
Surprise	Orangewood RV Center, 11449 W Bell Rd, 623-974-3000, free, access to water. Dump stations are located on the north and south side of propane tank. Total of three dump sites. 24/7 access. Latitude: 33.6386 • Longitude: -112.3063
Surprise	Van's RV-Trailer Company, 11565 W Bell Rd
Tempe	Apache Palms RV Park, 1836 E Apache Blvd # 9, 480-966-7399, $10
Tempe	RV Rental Outlet, 2165 E Apache Blvd, Tempe AZ 85281 / 480-461-0023. Located on block west of the 101 freeway. Open 9am-5:30pm Mon-Fri; 9am-2pm Sat; closed on Sunday. Latitude: 33.4146 • Longitude: -111.8931
Tucson	Nelson RV, 4324 N Flowing Wells Rd, 520-293-1010, fee not known.
Wickenburg	Shell Gas Station, 530 E Wickenburg Way, Wickenburg AZ 85390 / 520-684-1595. Cost is $5. Latitude: 33.9716 • Longitude: -112.7257
Yuma	Barney's Gas Station at intersection of 4th Ave and 29th St. If you purchase $20 worth of fuel, the fee to use dump station is $4; $8 without fuel purchase. Rinse water also available.
Yuma	Yuma Civic & Convention Center, 1440 Desert Hills Dr, 928-373-5040, $10. Closed weekends and some Fridays. Call ahead.

ARKANSAS

Below is a list of RV dump stations in Arkansas. Listed first are those easily accessed from Interstate highways followed by those in other locations throughout the state.

Interstate 30

Interstate 30 runs east to west from Interstate 40 in North Little Rock to the Texas state line. The highway is approximately 143 miles long. Eastbound travelers should read up the chart. Westbound travelers read down the chart.

Exit(mm)	Description
46	**AR 19 / Prescott**
	Love's Travel Stop
44	**AR 24 / Prescott**
	Rip Griffin Travel Center

Interstate 40

Interstate 40 is about 285 miles long. It runs east to west from the Tennessee state line to the Oklahoma state line. Eastbound travelers should read up the chart. Westbound travelers read down the chart.

Exit(mm)	Description
280	**Club Rd / Southland Dr / West Memphis**
	Flying J Travel Plaza
	Pilot Travel Center
	▼ *I-40 and I-55 run together / follows I-40 numbering* ▼
278	**AR 77 / 7th St / Missouri St / West Memphis**
	Flash Market
	▲ *I-40 and I-55 run together / follows I-40 numbering* ▲
233	**AR 261 / Palestine**
	Love's Travel Stop
193	**US 63 / AR 11 / to Hazen**
	T Ricks RV Park, 3001 Hwy 11N, 870-255-4914, $4
150	**Military Dr / Charles H Boyer Dr**
	Burns Park (city park), $5 fee. Dump is located in the campground south of the exit; follow signs to campground.

84	**US 64 / AR 331 / Russellville**
	Flying J Travel Plaza
	Ivys Cove RV Retreat, 321 Bradley Cove Rd, 479-747-3561, $10
	Pilot Travel Center
55	**US 64 / AR 109 / Clarksville**
	Highway 109 Truck Plaza

Interstate 55

Interstate 55 runs north to south for 72 miles from the Missouri state line to the Tennessee state line. A small stretch of I-55 in West Memphis is also I-40. Northbound travelers should read up the chart. Southbound travelers read down the chart.

Exit(mm)	Description
63	**US 61 / to Blytheville**
	Phoenix Truck Plaza
	▼ *I-40 and I-55 run together / follows I-40 numbering* ▼
278	**AR 77 / 7th St / Missouri St / West Memphis**
	Flash Market
	▲ *I-40 and I-55 run together / follows I-40 numbering* ▲
4	**King Dr / Southland Dr / West Memphis**
	Flying J Travel Plaza
	Pilot Travel Center

Interstate 530

Interstate 530 is about 46 miles long. It runs north to south from Little Rock to Pine Bluff. Northbound travelers should read up the chart. Southbound travelers read down the chart.

Exit(mm)	Description
34	**US 270 / White Hall**
	Big Red Travel Plaza

Other Locations

City or Town	Description
Berryville	Berryville RV Park (city park) on US 62 near the intersection with AR 21. Park is behind the Tourist Information Center and has 15 RV spaces with water, electricity, and sewage hookups for $16 per night. Donation requested for use of dump station. Phone: 870-423-3704
Hope	Fair Park (city park) off AR 174 at Park Dr
Horseshoe Bend	Box Hound Marina, 2 miles southeast of town via AR 289 and Tri-Lakes Dr. Also has an RV park, cabin rentals, and boat rentals.
Jacksonport	Jacksonport State Park on AR Hwy 69, three miles north of Newport, 870-523-2143.
North Little Rock	Downtown Riverside RV Park, 50 Riverfront Dr, North Little Rock AR 72114 / 501-340-5312. Cost is $5.
Pine Bluff	Hestand Stadium (district fairgrounds) at 420 N Blake St
Pine Bluff	Pine Bluff Convention Center at 500 E 8th Ave
Pine Bluff	Saracen Trace RV Park (city park) on US 65 Business (Martha Mitchell Expressway)
Pocahontas	Black River City Park on US 67 just south of town
Siloam Springs	Super 8 Motel at 1800 US 412W, $5 fee. Also has a 37 unit RV park with full hookups.

CALIFORNIA

Below is a list of RV dump stations in California. Listed first are those easily accessed from Interstate highways followed by those in other locations throughout the state.

Interstate 5

Interstate 5 runs north to south for approximately 797 miles from the Oregon state line to the Mexico border. Northbound travelers should read up the chart. Southbound travelers read down the chart.

Exit(mm)	Description
681b	**Market St / CA 273 / Southbound exit only**
	Exxon service station at southwest corner of N Market St and Caterpillar Rd
	Comments: Northbound travelers use Exit 680 (CA 299 / Lake Blvd) and go west to N Market St and then north to Caterpillar Rd.
670	**Riverside Ave / Anderson**
	Anderson RV Sales, 6040 State Highway 273, Anderson CA 96007 / 530-378-1993. Latitude: 40.4645 • Longitude: -122.3220
630	**South Ave / Corning**
	Flying J Travel Plaza, 2120 South Ave, 530-824-8767
	TA Travel Center
	Comments: Pass to right of propane tank, to left of gasoline islands. Dump is just beyond propane tank. Water supply is several feet from dump.
(608)	Willows Rest Area
537	**Main St / CA 113 S / Woodland**
	Bill Lowe's Tires, 801 East St, 530-666-2415, $10. From exit go west on Main St to East St and turn left (south).
	Comments: Dump available only during business hours, call. Must leave driver's license, pay fee and get key to unlock the lock on the dump hole lid. Dump is located on the east side of property along the tree line. Note: tree limbs are low. Fee may be waived for tire service customers.

Yolo County Fairgrounds at East St and Gibson Rd, 530-662-5393.
Comments: Enter fairgrounds on Gum Ave, north of Gibson Rd.
RV parking area is on right. RV parking is $25 per night with
full hookups or $20 per night with water and electric only.
Proceed south to fair gates, turn left to dump station near
fence and light poles. $20 fee if not a guest and only available
during business hours (8am-5pm, Mon-Fri).

485	**CA 12 / to Lodi**
	Flying J Travel Plaza
(445)	Westley Rest Area
407	**CA 33 / Santa Nella Village**
	TA Travel Center
257	**CA 58 / to Buttonwillow**
	TA Travel Center
219	**Laval Rd**
	Petro Stopping Center
	TA Travel Center
205	**Frazier Park**
	Flying J Travel Plaza
(204)	Tejon Pass Rest Area
167	**Lyons Ave / Pico Canyon Rd**
	Camping World, 24901 W Pico Canyon Rd, 800-235-3337 or 661-255-9220, free. Latitude: 34.3809 • Longitude: -118.5696
152	**Lankershim Blvd / Sun Valley**
	BenchMark RV, 11660 Tuxford St, 818-504-4813, $15, business hours only
110	**Harbor Blvd / Ball Rd / Anaheim**
	Anaheim Resort RV Park, 200 W Midway Dr, 714-774-3860. From exit follow Ball Rd east to Anaheim Blvd and then south to Midway Dr, turn right (west). A fee is charged.
96	**Sand Canyon Ave / Irvine**
	El Toro RV Service Center, $8
	McMahon RV at 6441 Burt Rd #10
91	**El Toro Rd / Lake Forest**
	Chevron gas station, $5; dump station is located next to the propane tanks on south end of lot.
79	**CA 1 / Pacific Coast Hwy / Camino Las Ramblas**
	Doheny State Beach, must pay day-use fee
(60)	Aliso Creek Rest Area

54c	**Oceanside Harbor Dr / Oceanside**
	Oceanside Harbor Boat Ramp, free
	Comments: On west side of harbor, circle around south side to approach, across from boat launch area, two stations in the lane
41b	**Encinitas Blvd**
	San Elijo State Beach, $10 fee
	Comments: From exit, follow Encinitas Blvd west to Pacific Coast Hwy 101, turn south and go approximately two miles to state beach
22	**Clairmont Dr / Mission Bay Dr / San Diego**
	Mission Bay Information Center, 2688 E Mission Bay Dr, San Diego CA 92109 / 619-276-8200. Free.
21	**Sea World Dr / San Diego**
	Public dump station at South Shores Boat Launch. From exit, follow Sea World Dr west to South Shores Boat Launch just before Sea World on right (north side of road). Latitude: 32.7620 • Longitude: -117.2142

Interstate 8

Interstate 8 runs east to west for 172 miles from the Arizona state line to Sunset Cliffs Blvd in San Diego. Eastbound travelers should read up the chart. Westbound travelers read down the chart.

Exit(mm)	Description
166	**CA 186 / Andrade Rd**
	Sleepy Hollow RV Park, 369 Andrade Rd, 760-572-5101, $5. Located 1.25 miles south of exit.
164	**Sidewinder Rd**
	Shell service station, 611 Sidewinder Rd, 760-572-2053. Fee varies.
115	**CA 86 / El Centro**
	Imperial 8 Travel Center
(108)	Sunbeam Rest Area
51	**Buckman Springs Rd**
	Buckman Springs Rest Area
20	**Greenfield Dr / El Cajon**
	Vacationer RV Resort, 1581 E Main St, 619-442-0904, $20

Interstate 10

Interstate 10 runs east to west for approximately 244 miles from the Arizona state line to CA 1 in Santa Monica. Eastbound travelers should read up the chart. Westbound travelers read down the chart.

Exit(mm)	Description
146	**Dillon Rd / Coachella**
	Love's Travel Stop, 760-775-3401, Latitude: 33.7187 • Longitude: -116.1685
104	**Apache Trail / Cabazon**
	Dump station is at the Shell gas station owned by Casino Morongo, 49750 Seminole Dr, 800-252-4499, $15 fee, free overnight parking allowed in casino parking lot.
76	**California St / Redlands**
	Mission RV Park, 26397 Redlands Blvd, 909-796-7570, south of exit, $10
50	**Mountain Ave / Ontario**
	Arrow Trailer Supply on W Holt Blvd, 909-986-3737, $5 fee, honor system for 24-hour operation.
	Comments: Arrow Trailer Supply is two miles south of exit. Dump station is on a side street, east side of store, just in from the curb.
	Green's Trailer Supply, 120 N Benson Ave, 909-983-1311, $3. Located one block north of Holt Blvd. Open Tue-Sat.
	Comments: Green's Trailer Supply is two miles south of exit.
45	**N Garey Ave / Pomona (westbound exit only)**
	KOA next to Fairplex, 2200 N White Ave, $10
	Comments: From exit go north one mile to Arrow Hwy; west to White Ave; south to KOA.
45a	**White Ave / Pomona (eastbound exit only)**
	KOA next to Fairplex, 2200 N White Ave, $10
	Comments: From exit go north 1.3 miles to KOA
44	**Dudley St / Fairplex Dr (westbound travelers)**
	East Shore RV Park, 1440 Camper View Rd, $5
	Comments: From exit go north on Fairplex Dr to Via Verde; west to Camper View Rd; north to RV park.
43	**Fairplex Dr / La Verne (eastbound travelers)**
	East Shore RV Park, 1440 Camper View Rd, $5
	Comments: From exit go north on Fairplex Dr to Via Verde; west to Camper View Rd; north to RV park.

Interstate 15

Interstate 15 runs north to south for about 292 miles from the Nevada state line to San Diego. Northbound travelers should read up the chart. Southbound travelers read down the chart.

Exit(mm)	Description
246	**CA 127 / Kelbaker Rd / Baker**
	Valero gas station on Baker Blvd, $5
178	**Lenwood Rd**
	Flying J Travel Plaza, 2611 Fisher Blvd
	Rip Griffin Travel Center
141	**Joshua St / US 395 / Hesperia**
	Newton's Outpost Cafe & Truck N Travel, $7. Key required; pick up at tire shop. Dump station is located at the truck wash/lube and brake stations directly facing I-15. Lots of parking for boondocking.
122	**Glen Helen Pkwy / Devore**
	Glen Helen Regional Park
	Comments: You must go to the main entrance to pay the $10 fee. The attendant will call a ranger to unlock the dump station, if necessary, and provide you with directions.
64	**Murrieta Hot Springs Rd / Murrieta**
	Murrieta Creek Boat & RV Storage, 25698 Adams Ave, Murrieta CA 92562 / 951-698-8577. Cost is $10. Latitude: 33.5417 • Longitude: -117.1950
	Temecula Valley RV, 26240 Jackson Ave, 951-894-2347, $5. From exit, go east about one mile to Jackson Ave, south to dealership. Latitude: 33.5455 • Longitude: -117.1755
58	**CA 79 S / Front St / Temecula**
	Pechanga Casino RV Park, $17. From I-15 go east to Pechanga Pkwy, turn right and go to casino on right. Stop at office to pay fee before using dump station. No potable water available.
43	**Old Hwy 395 / Escondido**
	Champagne Lakes RV Resort, 8310 Nelson Way, Escondido CA 92026 / 760-749-7572. Free if camping, otherwise cost is $10. RV resort is southeast of exit. Latitude: 33.2751 • Longitude: -117.1513
32	**CA 78 / Escondido**
	Freeway Trailer Sales, 945 W Mission Ave, 760-745-3970. Dump stations is at rear of RV and supplies shop; call during business hours. Fee is $10 for one time use, multi-use discount card available. From exit, go east one mile to Centre City Pkwy, south

one block to Mission Ave, right two blocks. Latitude: 33.1261 ·
Longitude: -117.0984

Interstate 80

Interstate 80 runs east to west for 208 miles from the Nevada state line
to 7th Street in San Francisco. Eastbound travelers should read up the
chart. Westbound travelers read down the chart.

Exit(mm)	Description
188	**CA 89 N / CA 267 S / Truckee** Coachland RV Park, 10100 Pioneer Trail, Truckee CA 96161 / 530-587-3071, $10
109	**Sierra College Blvd / Loomis** Loomis RV Park, 3945 Taylor Rd *Comments*: North on Sierra College Blvd to Taylor Rd and turn right, $7 fee
105a	**Atlantic St / Eureka Rd / Roseville** Chevron station at Rocky Ridge Dr and Eureka Rd. $4 fee or free with propane or fuel purchase.

Interstate 210

Interstate 210 begins on I-10 in Redlands and runs west to I-5 in San
Fernando. It is approximately 85 miles long. Eastbound travelers should
read up the chart. Westbound travelers read down the chart.

Exit(mm)	Description
36a	**I-605 / Huntington Dr / Duarte** Mount Olive Self Storage, 1500 Crestfield Dr, Duarte CA 91010 / 626-357-4330. Cost is unknown. Westbound I-210 travelers use Exit 36b. From exit, follow I-610 .4 mile to Huntington Dr, go E .2 mile then S .2 mile on Crestfield Dr. Call for hours of operation. Latitude: 34.1360 · Longitude: -117.9516
29a	**Sierra Madre Blvd / Pasadena (Westbound Exit)** Pasadena Propane Pro-Flame, 250 N Altadena Dr, 626-795-4359, $8.50 *Comments*: From exit, continue one block on E Maple St (parallel to the freeway) to Altadena Dr. Turn left (south) going under freeway. Turn left at Sierra Madre Blvd. Immediately turn

	right into driveway. It's best to call ahead if you plan to use this dump station.
28	**Altadena Ave / Pasadena (Eastbound Exit)**
	Pasadena Propane Pro-Flame, 250 N Altadena Dr, 626-795-4359, $8.50
	Comments: From exit, turn right (south) at light. Go south one block to Sierra Madre Blvd and turn left. Immediately turn right into driveway. It's best to call ahead if you plan to use this dump station.

Interstate 880

Interstate 880 in California runs north to south for about 46 miles from I-80 in Oakland to I-280 in San Jose. Northbound travelers should read up the chart. Southbound travelers read down the chart.

Exit(mm)	Description
15	**Durham Rd / Auto Mall Pkwy**
	Automall RV & Boat Storage, 42335 Boscell Rd, $10; located west of exit.

Other Locations

City or Town	Description
Arcata	From US 101, take the Valley West/Giuntoli Ln exit, north end of town. Turn east and go one block. Gas station is on southwest corner of Giuntoli Ln at first stop sign. Dump is on Valley West side of station near the car wash. $2 fee. A California welcome center is on other side of freeway at this exit.
Atwater	Castle Air Museum RV Park, Hospital Rd, Atwater CA 95301 / 209-388-1033. Cost is $5. Latitude: 37.3711 • Longitude: -120.5766
Baker	Tecopa Hot Springs County Park, 55 miles north of Baker via CA 127, in the center of Tecopa Hot Springs on west side of road
Bakersfield	Bakersfield Palms RV Park, $5. From CA 99 go east six miles on CA 58 to Fairfax Road; north 1/2 mile to RV park.
Bellflower	Affordable RV Storage, 8839 Park St, 562-633-3171, $20
Bishop	Large Shell truck/auto station at south end of town on US 395, double dump in back lot, $12 fee

Bodega Bay	Doran Park (county park), 707-875-3540, $5 (must pay day use fee to enter park - dumping is free). Camping also available.
Brawley	Rest area on CA 111, 6 miles north of town, very clean and well maintained
Calabasas	Malibu Creek State Park, 818-880-0367, south of US 101 via Las Virgenes Rd, dump station is located just outside the park entrance. Fee is the same amount that is charged for a day-use pass (currently $8).
Calipatria	Two Rivers Rest Area on CA 111, 2.5 miles south of town, water available, free. Latitude: 33.0817 • Longitude: -115.5232
Calistoga	Napa County Fairgrounds at 1435 Oak St, $2 fee
Cameron Park	Shell service station, 3405 Coach Ln, 530-677-9129. Take the Cameron Park Dr exit from US 50. $3 with 8 gallon fuel purchase or $5 without. Plenty of space to maneuver.
Carpinteria	Carpinteria State Beach, 5361 6th St, 805-648-2811, $8 entrance fee. From US 101, exit at the Casitas Pass Road and go west to Carpinteria Ave and turn right. Take your first left (Palm Ave) and follow to beach entrance.
Carson City	Altmans Winnebago, 22020 Recreation Rd, Carson City CA 90745 / 877-222-3246. Cost is $20 or $45 for assistance. Located off I-405 at Exit 34. Latitude: 33.8278 • Longitude: -118.2514
Chester	Enter via road and signs just west of Beacon gas station on south side of highway. Follow signs into older RV park. For larger RVs, recommend walking interior roads first; may involve backing out. $7.50 for dump, wash water, and fresh water (fresh water around front; again walk first).
Chowchilla	Arena Mobile Home Park, 203 S Chowchilla Blvd, 559-665-1752, $10
Clovis	ARCO Station, 1216 Clovis Ave, Clovis CA 93612 / 559-299-1130. Cost is $10. Open 5:30am to 9:30pm. On the southwest corner of Clovis and Barstow Ave. Latitude: 36.8153 • Longitude: -119.7003
Concord	Solano RV Storage off CA 4, 1701 Solano Way, 925-827-3177, $15. Buzzer on gate for manager. Open 9am to 6pm in summer and 9am to 5pm in winter. Closed major holidays and Thursdays.
Dinuba	Dinuba RV, 391 S Alta Ave, 559-591-3639, $5, open 8am-5pm, parts and service available.

Duncans Mills	Casini Ranch Family Campground, 22855 Moscow Rd, 707-865-2255, $5.50. Latitude: 38.4603 • Longitude: -123.0448
Ferndale	Humboldt County Fair, 1250 5th St, 707-786-9511, $3. Located behind Belotti Hall. Enter and pay on 5th St. Enter through main gate, turn immediate left then right where road ends; on left. Overnight camping with and without hookups available.
Fortuna	Shell gas station on Fortuna Blvd behind station in front of Safeway store, free
Fresno	Paul Evert's RV Country, 3633 S Maple Ave, Fresno CA 93725 / 559-486-1000. Free. Latitude: 36.6810 • Longitude: -119.7458
Gardena	Storage Etc. Self Storage, 740 W 190th St, Gardena CA 90248 / 310-933-5304. Cost is unknown. Latitude: 33.8601 • Longitude: -118.2874
Garden Grove	Elks Lodge at corner of Trask Ave and Newhope St. Also has 19 RV sites with electricity and water (members only). Accessed from the Garden Grove Freeway (CA 22) at Euclid St Exit. Dump is free to Elks members; $10 donation requested for non-members.
Gilroy	The Garlic Farm Center at US 101 and Monterey Rd, $5
Gilroy	Mount Madonna County Park, 408-842-2341, nine miles west of Gilroy or eight miles east of Watsonville via CA 152 (Hecker Pass Rd). 25-foot RV length limit. Fee unknown.
Goleta	76 gas station off US 101, $6
Grass Valley	Nevada County Fairgrounds near junction of CA 20 and CA 49. Follow fairground signs to gate #4. Unit is locked, call 530-273-6217 for times available or when attendant is on duty. $5 fee.
Grass Valley	Sierra Auto Center & U-Haul, $7. From Golden Center Freeway take the Brunswick Rd exit and go west to the old Nevada City Hwy. Turn south to Dorsey Dr. Continue past the signal light - on the right.
Grover Beach	Public dump station adjacent to Le Sage Golf Course near Pismo State Beach. Access from Le Sage Dr (off CA 1) or from Grand Ave before entrance to the beach. Drive through parking lot toward golf course and then bear right. Water available.
Hemet	Hemet Trailer Supply at 1371 W Acacia Ave (south of CA 74 and S Hamilton Ave intersection), $2 fee, dump

	open 24 hours, in a large parking area, always clean and functional
Hollister	RV Orchard Resort at Casa de Fruta, 10 miles north of Hollister on SR-152. 800-548-3813 or 408-842-9316. Cost is $10 if not a registered guest.
Huntington Beach	Bolsa Chica State Beach, $10 fee to get into beach parking area where dump is located. Camping is also available.
Independence	Fort Independence RV Park, 131 N Hwy 395, 760-878-3200, $10. Native American owned RV park on the west side of US 395 north of town. Dump station is behind the tribal office. Latitude: 36.8351 • Longitude: -118.2284
Indio	Wastewater Treatment Plant, 45500 Van Buren St, 760-347-2356
Jackson	Bear River Lake Resort, 40800 Hwy 88, 209-295-4868, $15. The resort campground is located 42 miles east of Jackson on CA 88. Open April thru October.
Joshua Tree	Joshua Tree Lake RV & Campground, 2601 Sunfair Rd, 760-366-1213, $4. Located four miles east of Park Blvd and five miles north on Sunfair Rd.
Lancaster	Dump is at the City of Lancaster National Soccer Field on Avenue L at 30th St E, north side of park, nice level pull through and non-potable water for flushing tanks, no fee. The dump station is on the north side of the east parking lot (not easy to find in this large facility). Washdown water furnished, but no drinking water. Closed 10pm to 6am.
Lee Vining	Mobil gas station on CA-120 about .25 mile west of US-395. Free with $20 fuel purchase or $5 without.
Lee Vining	Mono Vista RV Park, 57 Beaver Ln, 760-647-6401, fee not known. Campground is off US 395 in Lee Vining. Latitude: 37.9592 • Longitude: -119.1224
Lee Vining	Tuolumne Meadows Campground in Yosemite National Park. Dump station is on south side of highway about 1/2 mile west of gas station. Potable water available. Free.
Lemon Grove	Gas Stop at 7988 Broadway, $5 fee. Gas Stop is about 1/2 mile south of CA 94 Exit 8.
Lompoc	River Park (city park) adjacent to Santa Ynez River east of town (just east of Robinson Bridge on CA 246 and Sweeney Rd). Dump station is inside the park, beyond the campsites. The park (and dump station) close at dusk. $2
Mammoth Lakes	Convict Lake Campground (U.S. Forest Service), free. From US 395, follow Convict Lake Rd about two miles west to campground. Closed in winter. Potable water available.

Manteca	Manteca Trailer & Motorhome Inc, 1990 E Yosemite (CA 120), 209-239-1267, $10
Markleeville	Indian Creek Campground (BLM) on Airport Rd about 4 miles off CA 89. Gate to dump station is often closed - must get manager to open. $10
Menifee	Wilderness Lakes Resort, 30605 Briggs Rd, 951-672-4831, $5 fee. From Riverside take I-215 south. Two miles past Sun City, take the Newport Rd exit and go left 1.9 miles. Turn right at Briggs Rd and go .7 miles to entrance. Do not enter in store parking lot, proceed to second entrance.
Modesto	Chevron Station, 815 Kansas Ave, Modesto CA 95351 / 209-522-4610. Cost is $4 or free with fuel purchase. Latitude: 37.6460 • Longitude: -121.0180
Modesto	Ward's RV Storage, 141 E Orangeburg Ave, $2
Mojave	Red Rock Canyon State Park, 25 miles northeast of town on CA 14, fresh water available, $6 fee to enter park. Fee unknown for use of dump station.
Monrovia	Dry Dock RV Storage, 3131 S Peck Rd, 626-445-8762, $10. Site is just south of Live Oak Ave about three miles north of I-10 Exit 29.
Monterey	Monterey County Park at Laguna Seca Raceway about 3 miles east of Monterey on the north side of CA 68 ($6 fee). The dump is in the campground at the top of a very steep (12%) half-mile grade.
Morgan Hill	Parkway Lakes RV Park, 100 Ogier Ave, 408-779-0244, $12. Take the Bailey exit off US 101 and go west to Monterey Hwy. Go south two miles, campground is on left.
Napa	Skyline Wilderness Park (county park), 2201 Imola Ave, 707-252-0481, $5. Park closes at 7pm. Latitude: 38.2779 • Longitude: -122.2497
Newhall	Mobil gas station on San Fernando Rd, north of CA 14, $8
Niland	City park on west side of CA 111 near Main St, $3 fee
North Hollywood	Public dump station located at a small RV shop, 6730 Tujunga Ave, North Hollywood CA 91606. $20 for Class B/C, Travel Trailers; $25 Class A, Fifth Wheel Trailers. Open Mon-Fri, 8:30am-5:30pm; Sat, 9am-2pm; closed Sun.
Norwalk	Chevron station north of CA 91 freeway at Pioneer Blvd. Cost is $20.
Novato	Novato RV Park, 1530 Armstrong Ave, 415-897-1271, $10 fee. From US 101, take the San Marin Dr/Atherton Ave exit. Located about 25 miles north of the Golden Gate Bridge. Available to public during business hours Mon-Sun.

Oakdale	Tiger Express Chevron at 977 S Yosemite Blvd, $5 fee
Oceano	Dump station, trash, and water fill up near Pismo Beach. From US-101 at Exit 187A, follow Grand Ave west for 2.7 miles then go north .2 mile on Pacific Blvd and west .1 mile on Le Sage Dr. Cost is $10. Latitude: 35.1235 • Longitude: -120.6323
Old Station	US Forest Service Information Station near junction of CA 44 and CA 89. Not marked by roadway but easy to find; directly behind information station. $5 requested donation.
Olema	Olema Ranch Campground, 10155 State Hwy 1, 800-655-2267, $10. Dump is near the propane. Pay first at the campground general store. Nice place to camp, too.
Oxnard	McGrath State Beach on Harbor Blvd between Ventura and Oxnard, $8
Paso Robles	Chevron Station at SH-46 W, just south of town. Dump station is at the north end of the car wash. Fee unknown.
Paso Robles	Valero Gas Station, 2340 Spring St, Paso Robles CA 93446 / 805-238-3345. Cost is $10 or free with fuel purchase. Latitude: 35.6386 • Longitude: -120.6922
Perris	Lake Perris State Recreation Area, 17801 Lake Perris Dr, 951-657-0676. From I-215, take the Ramona Expy exit and go east about 2.5 miles. $8 entrance fee.
Petaluma	76 gas station off US 101 at Petaluma Blvd N, $9.50. The dump is at the rear of the gas station.
Playa del Rey	Dockweiler RV Park, 12001 Vista del Mar, 310-322-7036, 37-foot RV limit strictly enforced, $10 fee for dump station use. Camping is also available in this popular county park. Located adjacent to LAX airport off Imperial Highway. Latitude: 33.9309 • Longitude: -118.4349
Pleasanton	Alameda County Fairgrounds, 4501 Pleasanton Ave, Pleasanton CA 94566 / 925-426-7600. Cost is $25.
Quincy	Public dump station at RV park in Plumas County Fairground, 204 Fairground Rd, 530-283-6272, $10
Redwood City	Trailer Villa RV Park, 3401E Bayshore Rd, 650-366-7880, $10. From US 101, take the Marsh Rd exit and go north on Haven Ave to Bayshore Rd. Dump is open 24/7; instructions on office door for leaving fee after business hours.
Ridgecrest	Desert Empire Fairgrounds. There is a small RV park at the south end of the fairgrounds. The dump site is just north of the RV park. Lots of room to negotiate any size rig. $5

Ripon	Flying J Travel Plaza, 1501 N Jack Tone Rd, 209-599-4141, Free. Latitude: 37.7563 • Longitude: -121.1438
Ripon	Love's Travel Stop on CA 99 at Jack Tone Rd exit
Riverside	Riverside Regional Water Quality Treatment Plant, 5950 Acorn St, 951-351-6140, no charge. Open Mon-Fri, 7am-5pm; Sat, 12pm-4pm; closed Sun. Latitude: 33.9605 • Longitude: -117.4539
Roseville	Beal's Point Campground in the Folsom Lake State Recreation Area, $5. From I-80 Exit 103 (Douglas Blvd) go east about five miles to Auburn-Folsom Rd and then south two miles to park.
Salinas	Chevron station off US 101 at Laurel St exit, $5 for free with fill-up
Salyer	Rest Area on CA 299, very low water pressure.
San Francisco	Flyers Truck Stop, 400 Gateway Blvd, South San Francisco CA 94080. Cost is $5.
San Juan Capistrano	Caspers Wilderness Park (county park) about eight miles east of I-5 Exit 82 via Ortega Hwy (CA 74), $5. Latitude: 33.5342 • Longitude: -117.5495
San Jose	Arnone's RV Rentals, 186 San Jose Ave, San Jose CA 95125 / 408-297-0991. Cost is $15. From Highway 87 take the Curtner Ave exit and go east to Little Orchard; north to San Jose Ave; right to Arnone's RV Rentals.
San Jose	Family RV dealership, 2828 Monterey Rd, 408-365-1991, $25 fee, Mon-Sat 8am to 4pm. From US 101 use Tully Rd exit, west to Monterey Rd (CA 82), south to dealership.
San Lucas	Ultramar Beacon Truck Stop at US 101 and Wildhorse Rd between San Lucas and King City
Santa Barbara	Cachuma Lake Recreation Area (county park) on CA 154 about 20 miles northwest of town, 805-686-5054, $6
Santa Barbara	Marborg Industries, 136 N Quarantina, 800-798-1852, free. From US 101 take the Milpas St exit and travel north to Yanonali St and turn west. Go 2 blocks and then left into sanitation company. Easy in and out - no backing up.
Santa Clarita	Mobil gas station on San Fernando Rd, north of CA 14, 661-259-6682, $9
Santa Cruz	Steve's 76, 1500 Soquel Dr, Santa Cruz CA 95065 / 831-476-3857. Cost is $9 with purchase of fuel or LP. Open daily 6:30am to 10pm. Latitude: 36.9877 • Longitude: -121.9846
Santa Rosa	Rotten Robbie's gas station off US 101 at Todd Rd, 55 E Todd Rd, 707-584-9610, $10 or free with $10 merchandise purchase

Santa Rosa	Rosa Vista Trailer Park, 1885 Santa Rosa Ave, 707-544-6977, $5, no dumping after 8pm
Santee	Santee Lakes Recreation Preserve (municipal park), 9010 Carlton Oaks Dr, 619-596-3141. $10 fee. Camping also available.
Simi Valley	Oak Park (county park), 901 Quimisa, Simi Valley CA 93065 / 805-654-3951. Cost is $15 if not camping. Latitude: 34.2865 • Longitude: -118.8191
Simi Valley	Simi RV Wash & Service Center, 75 W Easy St, Simi Valley CA 93065 / 805-526-2002. $10 or free with purchase. Located near Costco off the CA-118 freeway. Easily accessed and a large fuel station for large RVs. Latitude: 34.2789 • Longitude: -118.8002
Simi Valley	Union 76 Station, 2605 Stearns St, Simi Valley CA 93063 / 805-522-0995. This service station is located just north of SR-118 at Stearns. Propane is available. Access to dump station may be tight for larger units. Cost is $10.
Sonoma	Shell service station on Broadway St one block south of town square. Dump is on left side of station. Plenty of room to get in and out. $10
Thousand Oaks	Majestic RV Center, 3242 Thousand Oaks Blvd, 805-496-1133, $8. Latitude: 34.1685 • Longitude: -118.8338
Tipton	Rest Area on CA 99, north of town, no fee, good clean water
Torrance	Meyer's RV, 433 Alaska Ave, 310-328-1515, $8. From I-405 Exit 39, go south on Crenshaw Blvd about two miles to Maricopa St. Turn right (west) to Alaska Ave and turn right (north). Latitude: 33.8426 • Longitude: -118.3333
Tulare	Phillip S. Raine Rest Area on CA 99 at Avenue 176, south of Tulare, no charge
Tulelake	Public dump station across from True Hardware off CA 139 at Modoc Ave and D St, no charge
Turlock	Chevron gas station off CA 99 at the Los Banos/Lander Ave exit, $5 charge. Very courteous, easy to approach, and clean.
Twain	State Route 70 (Feather River), sign on highway. Pay $4 at office; unlock drain and return key. Fresh water a few feet ahead from spigot on small building.
Valley Springs	Public dump stations in campgrounds at New Hogan Lake (Corps of Engineers) about 1.5 miles southeast of Valley Springs via CA 26 and Hogan Dam Rd. Open year-round. $6

Van Nuys	76 Station at corner of White Oak Ave and Sherman Way. From I-405, take the Sherman Way exit and go west 2.5 miles. From US 101 (Ventura Freeway), take the White Oak Ave exit and go north 2 miles. $15. Latitude: 34.2009 • Longitude: -118.5187
Ventura	Ventura Beach RV Resort, 800 W Main St, 805-643-9137, $15. Northbound US 101 travelers use the California St exit; southbound travelers use the Main St exit.
Victorville	Mojave Narrows Regional Park (county park), 18000 Yates Rd, 760-245-2226, $5 fee. Can be reached from I-15 exit 147 (Bear Valley Rd) by traveling east four miles and then north on Ridge Crest Rd two miles to Yates Rd.
Visalia	Visalia RV Sales & Service, 6603 Betty Dr, 559-651-2300, $3 fee or free with purchase from their store. Hours: Mon-Fri 8am-5pm; Sat 9am-4:30pm. Latitude: 36.3516 • Longitude: -119.4233
Watsonville	Mount Madonna County Park, 408-842-2341, nine miles west of Gilroy or eight miles east of Watsonville via CA 152 (Hecker Pass Rd). 25-foot RV length limit. Fee unknown.
Watsonville	Pinto Lake Park (city park), 451 Green Valley Rd, 831-722-8129, $5 fee. From CA 1, take Green Valley Road exit and go thru 6 lights, last crossroad is Airport Blvd, go 1/2 mile and turn left
Westminster	Springdale Self Serve Car Wash, 13095 Springdale St, 714-373-1182, $10
Willits	KOA, 1600 Hwy 20, 707-459-6179, $10
Yountville	Veterans Home of California - Yountville at CA 29 and California Dr. Check at guard station, then a short drive to the RV park. $5
Yucaipa	Yucaipa Regional Park, 33900 Oak Glen Rd, 909-790-3127, $10. Campground has 26 full-hookup sites for about $27 per night.
Yucca Valley	Desert Sky Motel, 55492 29 Palms Hwy (CA 62), $18 (additional fee for water)
Yucca Valley	Black Rock Campground in Joshua Tree National Park, donation requested. From CA 62 in town, follow Joshua Ln to its end and turn right for one block and then south to campground. Latitude: 34.0742 • Longitude: -116.3875

COLORADO

Below is a list of RV dump stations in Colorado. Listed first are those easily accessed from Interstate highways followed by those in other locations throughout the state.

Interstate 25

Interstate 25 runs north to south for about 300 miles from the Wyoming state line to the New Mexico state line. Northbound travelers should read up the chart. Southbound travelers read down the chart.

Exit(mm)	Description
269b	**CO 14 / E Mulberry St / Fort Collins**
	Fort Collins CoOp, no fee
	Comments: CoOp is on NW Service Road, just north of CO 14. Dump station is free but the business appreciates you buying fuel or other items if you use dump.
254	**CR 16 / near Loveland**
	Johnson's Corner RV Park, 3618 SE Frontage Rd, Loveland CO 80537 / 970-669-8400. $15 Latitude: 40.3545 • Longitude: -104.9812
184	**Meadows Parkway / US 85**
	Town of Castle Rock Service Center, 4175 N Castleton Ct, 720-733-2477, free
	Comments: From exit, go west to Santa Fe Dr and turn south (left), follow to Justice Way and turn east (left). Watch for one story brick building on right, go thru gate, dump is on right, open Mon-Fri 8am to 4pm
161	**CO 105 / Woodmoor Dr / Monument**
	Colorado Heights Campground east side of I-25 on Monument Hill Rd, 8am to 8pm, $10
139	**US 24 Bypass / Colorado Springs**
	Pikes Peak Traveland, 719-596-2716, $8. From exit go east to Academy Blvd. Go north on Academy Blvd to Platte Ave and then east one mile. Dump station available during business hours only.
138	**Circle Dr / Colorado Springs**
	Shell/Circk K store on the northeast corner of I-25 and Circle Dr. Free with fillup, $5 otherwise.

Interstate 70

Interstate 70 runs east to west for 447 miles from the Kansas state line to the Utah state line. Eastbound travelers should read up the chart. Westbound travelers read down the chart.

Exit(mm)	Description
(437)	Welcome Center (wb)
405	**CO 59 / Seibert**
	Shady Grove Campground, 306 Colorado Ave, 970-664-2218, $5 fee
285	**Airport Blvd**
	Flying J Travel Plaza
266	**CO 72 / W 44th Ave / Wheat Ridge**
	Prospect RV Park, 11600 W 44th Ave, 303-424-4414, $10
163	**Edwards / to US 6**
	Rest Area
90	**CO 13 / Rifle**
	Rest Area
	Comments: From exit, go north and follow rest area signs. Dump is located on the right as you exit the rest area.
26	**US-50 / Grand Junction**
	Mobile City RV Park, 2322 Hwy 6 & 50, Grand Junction CO 81505 / 970-242-9291. Cost is unknown. From I-70 Exit 26 follow US-50 southeast 1.5 miles. Latitude: 39.1000 • Longitude: -108.6232
19	**CO 340 / Fruita**
	Welcome Center
	Monument RV Resort, 607 Hwy 340, Fruita CO 81521 / 970-858-3155. Cost is $8. From I-70 Exit 19 go south about 1/2 mile to park.

Interstate 76

Interstate 76 runs east to west from the Nebraska state line to I-70 in Denver. It is about 184 miles long. Eastbound travelers should read up the chart. Westbound travelers read down the chart.

Exit(mm)	Description
180	**US 385 / Julesburg**
	Welcome Center

125	**US 6 / Sterling**
	Rest Area
31	**SR-52 / Hudson**
	Love's Travel Stop, 201 E Colorado Hwy 52, Hudson CO 80642 / 303-536-9900. Free.
22	**E 152nd Ave / E Bromley Ln / Brighton**
	Co-op at 55 W Bromley Ln, $5. From exit travel west about 4 miles to Co-op.

Interstate 225

Interstate 225 in Colorado is 12 miles long. It primarily runs north to south, connecting I-70 Exit 282 with I-25 Exit 200.

Exit(mm)	Description
4	**CO 83 / Parker Rd / Aurora**
	Cherry Creek State Park, 4201 S Parker Rd, Aurora CO 80014 / 303-690-1166. Fee is based on current camping and day-use fees (currently over $20).

Other Locations

City or Town	Description
Almont	Public dump station in the Taylor Park area of Gunnison National Forest. From the Taylor Park Reservoir, follow CR 55 southeast about four miles to station. Fee-honor system, not attended. Serves camping in the Taylor Park area. $7. Latitude: 38.813 • Longitude: -106.547
Antonito	Conoco gas station on US 285 in town, $4 fee.
Bayfield	Bayfield Riverside RV Park, 41743 US-160, Bayfield CO 81122 / 970-884-2475. Cost is $8. Latitude: 37.2297 • Longitude: -107.6070
Buena Vista	KOA campground, 27700 County Road 303, 719-395-8318, located on US 285 about one mile east of US 24 and US 285 junction, $15 fee. Latitude: 38.8151 • Longitude: -106.0914
Buena Vista	Snowy Peaks RV Park on US 24, north end of town, $10 fee if not camping
Cortez	City Service Center, 110 W Progress Cir, Cortez CO 81321 / 970-565-7320. Closed in winter. Latitude: 37.3693 • Longitude: -108.5884

Canon City	Shell, 420 Royal Gorge Blvd, Canon City CO 81212 / 719-372-3200. Cost is $5. Latitude: 38.4394 • Longitude: -105.2406
Canon City	Conoco, 2801 E Main St, Canon City CO 81212 / 719-276-3333. Free with fuel purchase. Latitude: 38.4470 • Longitude: -105.2067
Craig	Moffat County Fairgrounds on east end of town. Turn south off US 40 at east end of fairgrounds and go about one block and turn left.
Creede	City dump station along CO 149, west side of town; small sign in tree. Look for blue steel building beyond ball park's center field. City drinking water from hydrant reasonably separated. $3 to $5 donation requested.
Del Norte	A public dump station is at 1st and Spruce streets
Delta	Delta Chamber of Commerce on 3rd St between Main and Palmer. Turn west off Main St onto 3rd St, go 3/4 block, enter parking lot on left, dump is at end of lot. Free.
Dove Creek	Dove Creek Superette, 445 US Hwy 491, Dove Creek CO 81324 / 970-677-2336. Free. Latitude: 37.7663 • Longitude: -108.9131
Estes Park	Stanley Park Fairgrounds east of town off Community Drive. Entrance is directly across from ball fields. Cost is $15; fresh water available. The dumps are locked until you pay at the fairgrounds office, a few hundred feet away. Best access from town: head east out of the downtown area on US-36 toward Boulder. Just before crossing the lake, turn right onto Community Dr, then another right into fairgrounds. The dump is on the right. Latitude: 40.3718 • Longitude: -105.4996
Evans	Evans C-Store at 665 US 85 in Evans
Florence	Public dump station at gas station on corner of Hwy-50 and Hwy-115. Fee not known.
Fort Collins	Fort Collins Lakeside KOA, 1910 N Taft Hill Rd, 970-484-9880, $20 or free if you're a guest. Latitude: 40.6145 • Longitude: -105.1137
Frisco	Breckenridge Sanitation Plant next to the Blue River Inlet on Dillon Reservoir about 3 miles east of Frisco via SR-9. Cost is $5.
Greeley	Missile Site Park, 10611 Spur 257, 970-381-7451. Park is off US 34 Bus west of town and also has 20 campsites for $5 per night.

Holly	Rest area on US 50 (south side of road) about two miles east of town. Free
Hooper	My Sister's Place at 11704 CO 17
Lake George	Travel Port RV Park on US 24 in Lake George, which is between Colorado Springs and Buena Vista. $10 fee if you are not camping.
Lamar	Lamar Truck Plaza at US 50 and US 287
Lamar	Love's Travel Stop at US 50 and US 287
Leadville	City of Leadville Sanitation on the south side of US 24 near the Colorado Mountain College. $5 fee.
Littleton	Chatfield State Park off US 85 or CO 470, $5. Water is turned off between Labor Day and Memorial Day.
Littleton	Lawn Irrigation Design Center, 9966 W Bowles Ave, Littleton CO 80123 / 303-979-3400. Cost is $8. Open Mon-Sat, 8am-6:30pm; Sun, 10am-4pm.
Longmont	Boulder County Fairgrounds one block east of Hover Rd and Rogers Rd/Boston Ave intersection, $5 fee. The fairground also has several RV sites. Open daily from 8am to 4pm. 303-678-6235
Louisville	Louisville Recycle Center on CO 42 just north of Pine St. Dumping is free. Coin-operated water service is available.
Lyons	Library Park on US 36 one block east of US 36 and CO 7 junction. Not readily visible. It's across the street from the visitor center.
Meeker	Public dump station is at 6th and Water streets
Monte Vista	Monte Vista Co-op on US 160 on eastern edge of town. Dump is near the diesel fuel pumps. Fresh water available at nearby rodeo grounds. To reach rodeo grounds, go west on US 160 then double-back right to the east on Sherman St (poorly signed). Proceed east on Sherman St; north on Sky High Trail; east on Clearview Dr. Watch for three high, freeze-proof water hydrants on the left side.
Montrose	Country Village RV Resort, 22045 S US 550, 7 miles south of town, $5 fee if not camping
Nathrop	Chalk Creek Campground on US 285 about 5 miles south of US 24 and US 285 junction. $20 fee if not camping.
Ordway	The Junction at CO 71 and CO 96
Pagosa Springs	Public dump station at the Giant Gas Station. Non-potable water available for cleaning hose.

Pueblo West	Shell, 101 S McCulloch Blvd, Pueblo West CO 81007 / 719-547-1770. Free. Gas station is near southwest corner of US-50 and McCulloch Blvd, 7 miles west of I-25 Exit 101. Dump station is on the north side of site, next to the car wash. Latitude: 38.3330 • Longitude: -104.7445
Rangely	Rangely Camping Park, $5. Park is at the east end of town; turn north off CO 64 at the blue fire station, then turn right in two blocks.
Rocky Ford	A public dump station is at the Loaf'n Jug on US 50 in center of town. $5 fee, free with fuel purchase.
Salida	Salida Chamber of Commerce on east side of the Hot Springs Pool park, right outside the chamber, donations accepted.
Silverthorne	Blue River Treatment Plant, three miles north of I-70 on CO-9. Free to customers of the Silverthorne/Dillon Joint Authority, otherwise $3 for RVs and $5 for busses. Open 7:30am to 5:00pm, Sun thru Fri (Sat and holiday hours vary). 970-468-6152
Telluride	Public dump station in the public parking lot at Mahoney Dr and W Pacific Ave, free. From CO 145, go one block south on Mahoney Dr and turn right. Water is available. Open until 6pm.
Walden	KOA campground on CO 14 about 16 miles southeast of town, $5 fee
Walden	Public dump station at 3rd and Washington, across from city pool, one block east of CO 125, donation accepted
Westcliffe	Public dump station on the south side of city park. City park is on Hermit St between 3rd and 4th. No charge. Latitude: 38.1310 • Longitude: -105.4663

CONNECTICUT

Below is a list of RV dump stations in Connecticut. Listed first are those easily accessed from Interstate highways followed by those in other locations throughout the state.

Interstate 84

Interstate 84 runs east to west for 98 miles from the Massachusetts state line to the New York state line. Exit numbers are based on the consecutive numbering system rather than the mile marker system. Eastbound travelers should read up the chart. Westbound travelers read down the chart.

Exit(mm)	Description
(85)	Welcome Center (wb)
58	**Roberts St / East Hartford**
	Cabela's, 475 E Hartford Blvd N, East Hartford CT 06118 / 860-290-6200. Free. Latitude: 41.7535 • Longitude: -72.6201
(42)	Rest Area (eb); Dump station is closed Nov-Apr
2	**US 6 / US 202 / Old Ridgebury Rd**
	Welcome Center (eb)

Interstate 91

Interstate 91 runs north to south for 58 miles from the Massachusetts state line to I-95 in New Haven. Exit numbers are based on the consecutive numbering system rather than the mile marker system. Northbound travelers should read up the chart. Southbound travelers read down the chart.

Exit(mm)	Description
(22)	Rest Area (nb)
(15)	Rest Area (sb)

Other Locations

City or Town	Description
none	none at this time

DELAWARE

Below is a list of RV dump stations in Delaware. Listed first are those easily accessed from Interstate highways followed by those in other locations throughout the state.

Interstate

There are no listings for Interstate highways in Delaware at the present time. If you know of a site that should be listed, please visit our web site and complete the "Add a Dump Station" form.

Exit(mm)	Description
none	none at this time

Other Locations

City or Town	Description
Bear	Lum's Pond State Park, 1068 Howell School Rd, 302-368-6989, $7 or free if camping. Park is south of US 40 via US 301/DE 896
Dover	Dover Air Force Base at Bay Rd/Hwy 1 in FamCamp, southeast of the Christmas tree and Transient Ramp. Must have Military/DOD ID to get on base. $3
Dover	Dover Downs Casino at 1131 N DuPont Hwy (US 13), no fee
Felton	Killens Pond State Park, 302-284-3412, $7 (honor system when ranger not present). From Felton go south on US 13 to Paradise Alley Rd and then east to the park's campground entrance.
Seaford	Wastewater treatment facility at Pine St and King St
Smyrna	Rest area north of town on US 13, $10 fee, also accessible from DE 1 Exit 119

FLORIDA

Below is a list of RV dump stations in Florida. Listed first are those easily accessed from Interstate highways followed by those in other locations throughout the state.

Interstate 4

Interstate 4 runs east to west for 134 miles from I-95 in Daytona Beach to I-275 in Tampa. Eastbound travelers should read up the chart. Westbound travelers read down the chart.

Exit(mm)	Description
55	**US-27 / to Haines City**
	Fort Summit KOA, 2525 Frontage Rd, Lake Buena Vista FL 32830 / 863-424-1880. Fee unknown. Open 24/7
44	**FL 559 / to Auburndale**
	Love's Travel Stop
10	**CR 579 / Mango / Thonotosassa**
	Travel Centers of America, 813-262-1560, free. Latitude: 27.9921 • Longitude: -82.2863
7	**US 301 / Hillsborough Ave**
	Singh 301

Interstate 10

Interstate 10 runs east to west for 370 miles from I-95 in Jacksonville to the Alabama state line. Eastbound travelers should read up the chart. Westbound travelers read down the chart.

Exit(mm)	Description
303	**US 441 / Lake City**
	Lake City Campground, $15 fee, one mile north of exit.
258	**FL 53 / Madison**
	Yogi Bear's Jellystone Park & RV Resort, $8 fee
	Comments: From exit, go south 200 feet to Old Saint Augustine Rd and then west about 1 mile to park
192	**US 90 / to Tallahassee**
	Camping World, 31300 Blue Star Hwy, Midway FL 32343 / 800-446-3199. Latitude: 30.5029 • Longitude: -84.4521

Flying J Travel Plaza

Pilot Truck Stop, free. Dump station is adjacent to the large propane tank to the north of the building with plenty of turning room.

31	**FL 87 / to Milton**	
	KOA north of exit, $10 fee	

Interstate 75

Interstate 75 runs north to south for 472 miles from the Georgia state line to the junction with FL 826 in Miami. Northbound travelers should read up the chart. Southbound travelers read down the chart.

Exit(mm)	Description
368	**CR 318 / Orange Lake**
	Petro Stopping Center
285	**FL 52 / to Dade City**
	Flying J Travel Plaza
210	**SR-780 / Fruitville Rd / Sarasota**
	Sun-N-Fun, 7125 Fruitville Rd, Sarasota FL 34240 / 800-843-2421. $10. Resort is 1.2 miles east of exit. Latitude: 27.3384 • Longitude: -82.4268
9a	**FL 820 / Pines Blvd / Pembroke Pines**
	C.B. Smith Park (county park), 900 N Flamingo Rd, 954-437-2650. Camping is also available.

Interstate 95

Interstate 95 runs north to south for 382 miles from the Georgia state line to US 1 in Miami. Northbound travelers should read up the chart. Southbound travelers read down the chart.

Exit(mm)	Description
305	**FL 206 / to Hastings**
	Flying J Travel Plaza
273	**US 1**
	Love's Travel Stop, 386-671-9585
131b	**FL 68 / Orange Ave**
	Flying J Travel Plaza

31	**FL 816 / Oakland Park Blvd / Oakland Park**
	Easterlin Park (county park), 1000 NW 38th St, 954-938-0610. Camping is also available.
21	**FL 822 / Sheridan St / Hollywood**
	Topeekeegee Yugnee Park (county park), 3300 N Park Rd, 954-985-1980. Camping is also available.

Other Locations

City or Town	Description
Arcadia	Peace River Campground, 2998 NW Hwy 70, Arcadia FL 34266 / 800-559-4011. Cost is $8. Latitude: 27.2281 · Longitude: -81.8917
Bahia Honda Key	Bahia Honda State Park, 36850 Overseas Hwy, Big Pine Key FL 33043 / 305-872-2353. Cost is $6 for non-registered guests. There is a centralized dump station in the Buttonwood Camping Area of the state park. Latitude: 24.6587 · Longitude: -81.2770
Brooksville	Register Chevrolet, 14181 Cortez Blvd, 352-597-3333. Location along westbound FL 50 across from Register RV. Free. Closed on Sundays. Available during business hours only.
Clewiston	John Stretch Park on US 27 about 9 miles east of town at Lake Harbor, free. Dump station is between public restrooms and highway near pump station at east entrance to park.
Gainesville	Public dump station east of Waldo Rd on NE 39th Ave near Alachua County Fairgrounds. Turn in at the Agricultural Extension Office and it is immediately on the left.
Kissimmee	Camp USA RV Rentals & Service, 4560 Old Tampa Hwy, 888-647-6665, $35. Near Disney World. Latitude: 28.2583 · Longitude: -81.4644
Lake City	October Bend RV Park, 2960 SE October Rd, Lake City FL 32025 / 352-317-1326. Cost is unknown. From I-75 Exit 414, follow US 41 north to CR 238 and turn right. At SE October Rd, turn right and follow to campground. The RV park is about 3.5 miles from exit. Latitude: 29.9671 · Longitude: -82.5732
Lakeland	Lakeland Civic Center, 701 W Lime St, Free. Dump station is on the west side of civic center's parking lot. Wash down water available.

Miami	Larry & Penny Thompson Park (county park) campground, 12451 SW 184th St (Eureka Dr), about one mile west of West Dade Expy (FL 821). Cost is $10.
Navarre	Emerald Beach RV Park, 8885 Navarre Pkwy (US 98), 850-939-3431, $10 fee
Ochopee	Midway Campground on south side of US 41 near Fiftymile Bend in Big Cypress National Preserve. $6 or $3 with Golden Age Passport.
Ochopee	Public dump station near the Big Cypress National Preserve Headquarters on US 41, $6 or $3 with Golden Age Passport
Ohio Key	Sunshine Key Resort on US 1, $10 fee, 305-872-2217
Palm Harbor	Sherwood Forest RV Park, 175 Alt US 19 S, 727-784-4582, $5
Panama City Beach	PineGlen RV Park on US 98 about 4 miles east of FL 79, just before Alf Coleman Rd. $10
Patrick Air Force Base	Family Camp at Patrick Air Force Base has a free dump station and water. You must have a military ID to get on post. Enter the base via the A1A Highway truck gate.
Port Richey	Suncoast RV Resort, 9029 US Hwy 19, $10. Resort is on west side of road three miles south of FL Hwy 52 and the GulfView Square Mall.
Sunrise	Markham Park (county park), 16001 W State Road 84, 954-389-2000. Camping is also available. Park is located near the junction of I-75 and I-595.
Thonotosassa	Hillsborough River State Park, 15402 US 301N, 813-987-6771, $4 entrance fee. Latitude: 28.1450 • Longitude: -82.2255
Tierra Verde	Fort De Soto Park, 3500 Pinellas Baway S, Tierra Verde FL 33715 / 727-582-2267. Donation (box is located in the park office). There are two dump stations. One is just left of the office; this one is a tight turn with overhanging trees. The other one is just past the camp store on the left. It has a nice turning radius and is easier to use.

GEORGIA

Below is a list of RV dump stations in Georgia. Listed first are those easily accessed from Interstate highways followed by those in other locations throughout the state.

Interstate 16

Interstate 16 runs east to west for 167 miles from Savannah to I-75 in Macon. Eastbound travelers should read up the chart. Westbound travelers read down the chart.

Exit(mm)	Description
49	**GA 257 / to Dublin**
	Love's Travel Stop, 3009 Highway 257, 478-296-1368
(46)	Rest Area (wb)
(44)	Rest Area (eb)

Interstate 20

Interstate 20 runs east to west for 202 miles from the South Carolina state line to the Alabama state line. Eastbound travelers should read up the chart. Westbound travelers read down the chart.

Exit(mm)	Description
(201)	Welcome Center (wb)
(103)	Rest Area (eb)
37	**Fairburn Rd / Douglasville**
	John Bleakley RV Center, 6200 Fairburn Rd, 770-949-4500, free. Dump station open during business hours (Mon-Fri: 8am-6pm; Sat: 8am-5pm). Use of dump station is for out-of-state travelers and John Bleakley RV Center customers.
9	**Atlantic Ave / Waco**
	Love's Travel Stop, 770-824-5040

Interstate 75

Interstate 75 runs north to south for 355 miles from the Tennessee state line to the Florida state line. Northbound travelers should read up the chart. Southbound travelers read down the chart.

Exit(mm)	Description
326	**Carbondale Rd**
	Pilot Travel Center
320	**GA 136 / Resaca / to Lafayette**
	Flying J Travel Plaza
(319)	Rest Area (sb)
296	**Cassville-White Rd**
	TA Travel Center
201	**GA 36 / to Jackson**
	Flying J Travel Plaza
135	**US 41 / GA 127/ Perry**
	Perry Welcome Center, 101 General Courtney Hodges Blvd, free
(118)	Rest Area (sb)
(108)	Rest Area (nb)
101	**US 280 / GA 90 / Cordele**
	Pilot Travel Center
(85)	Rest Area (nb)
(76)	Rest Area (sb)
60	**Central Ave / Tifton**
	Pilot Travel Center
(48)	Rest Area (sb)
(47)	Rest Area (nb)
11	**GA 31 / Valdosta**
	Wilco Travel Plaza
5	**GA 376 / Lake Park**
	Eagles Roost RV Resort on Mill Store Rd, $5
2	**Lake Park / Bellville**
	Flying J Travel Plaza

Interstate 85

Interstate 85 runs north to south for 179 miles from the South Carolina state line to the Alabama state line. Northbound travelers should read up the chart. Southbound travelers read down the chart.

Exit(mm)	Description
160	**GA 51 / to Homer**
	Flying J Travel Plaza
	Petro Stopping Center
101	**Indian Trail Lilburn Rd / Norcross**
	Jones RV Park, 2200 Willow Trail Pkwy, Norcross GA 30093 / 770-923-0911. Cost is $10. Latitude: 33.9255 • Longitude: -84.1765
(.5)	Welcome Center (nb)

Interstate 95

Interstate 95 runs north to south for 113 miles from the South Carolina state line to the Florida state line. Northbound travelers should read up the chart. Southbound travelers read down the chart.

Exit(mm)	Description
102	**US 80 / GA 26 / Pooler**
	Bill Waites RV World; go east of exit and then right at first light; no charge
3	**GA 40 / Kingsland / to Saint Marys**
	Pilot Travel Center
1	**Saint Marys Rd**
	Cisco Travel Plaza

Interstate 185

Interstate 185 is about 48 miles long. It runs north to south between I-85 near La Grange and US 27 south of Columbus. Northbound travelers should read up the chart. Southbound travelers read down the chart.

Exit(mm)	Description
12	**Williams Rd / Columbus**
	Welcome Center, 1751 Williams Rd, Columbus GA 31904 / 706-649-7455. Free.

Interstate 475

Interstate 475 runs north to south for 16 miles. It begins on I-75 at exit 177 and ends at I-75 exit 156, bypassing Macon. Northbound travelers should read up the chart. Southbound travelers read down the chart.

Exit(mm)	Description
(8)	Rest Area (nb)

Other Locations

City or Town	Description
Bainbridge	Inland Travel Center on US 84 just west of Bainbridge at US 27
McCaysville	Rebel's Chevron on GA 5 between Blue Ridge and McCaysville. The dump station is close to the diesel pump and phone booth on the right side of the driveway as you pull in. Cost is $10.
Pelham	Amoco at 317 US 19
Rincon	Whispering Pines RV Park, 1755 Hodgeville Road, Rincon GA 31326 / 912-728-7562. $10 charge for non-residents.
Thomasville	Thomasville Travel Center at 2685 US 84 Bypass
Washington	Callaway Plantation Museum on US 78 five miles west of town, 706-678-2013, free. Site is open Tue thru Sat 10am to 5pm, Sun 12:30pm to 3:30pm. RV camping available.
Waynesboro	City park off US 25, south end of town, no fee

HAWAII

Below is a list of RV dump stations in Hawaii.

Other Locations

City or Town	Description
Hilo	County wastewater treatment plant, 108 Railroad Ave, 808-961-8338, free.

IDAHO

Below is a list of RV dump stations in Idaho. Listed first are those easily accessed from Interstate highways followed by those in other locations throughout the state.

Interstate 15

Interstate 15 runs north to south for 196 miles from the Montana state line to the Utah state line. Northbound travelers should read up the chart. Southbound travelers read down the chart.

Exit(mm)	Description
167	**ID 22 / Dubois**
	Scoggins RV Camp
119	**Grandview Dr / US 20 / Idaho Falls**
	Grandview Texaco
118	**US 20 / W Broadway St / Idaho Falls**
	South Tourist Park (city park), 2800 S Yellowstone Hwy, no charge. Free overnight RV parking (limit one night). Latitude: 43.4714 • Longitude: -112.0574
113	**US 26 / to Idaho Falls**
	Targhee Inn & RV, 6805 S Overland Dr, 208-523-1960, $5. Latitude: 43.4374 • Longitude: -112.1182
108	**E 1250 N / Horseshoe Rd / Shelley**
	North Bingham Recreation Site (County Park)
93	**US 26 / ID 39 / Blackfoot**
	Chevron on Parkway Dr
71	**Pocatello Creek Rd / Pocatello**
	Bannock County Fairgrounds
	Comments: From exit go east on Pocatello Creek Rd, north on Olympus Dr, and west on Fairway Dr.
	Willie's Chevron
47	**US 30 / McCammon / to Lava Hot Springs**
	McCammon Chevron
31	**ID 40 / to Downey**
	Flags West Truck Stop (fee charged)

Interstate 84

Interstate 84 runs east to west for approximately 276 miles from the Utah state line to the Oregon state line. Eastbound travelers should read up the chart. Westbound travelers read down the chart.

Exit(mm)	Description
216	**ID 77 / ID 25 / to Declo**
	Village of Trees RV Resort at Travel Stop (fee charged)
208	**ID 27 / to Burley**
	Cassia County Fairgrounds, just north of intersection of US 30 and Hiland Ave, free
194	**ID 25 / to Hazelton**
	Greenwood Pioneer Stop (fee charged)
168	**ID 79 / to Jerome**
	Honker's Mini Mart
157	**ID 46 / Wendell**
	Burt Harbaugh Motors on N Idaho St (ID 46), 1 mile north of exit
	Intermountain Motor Homes & RV Park at 1894 Frontage Rd
	RV dump station maintained by the city at 210 S Shohone St, one block west of N Idaho St (ID 46)
	Wendell Gas & Oil
71	**Orchard / Mayfield**
	Boise Stage Stop
54	**US 20 / US 26 / Broadway Ave / Boise**
	Flying J Travel Plaza, 3353 S Federal Way, 208-385-9745
	Comments: Dump is located in an alley between Flying J's main store and a diesel repair shop behind it. There is a large sign painted on the building indicating its location. The dump is fenced in, but it is free. Give your ID to the clerk, sign a ledger, and they will give you the key. Rinse water is available; potable water and air are available nearby.
36	**Franklin Blvd / Nampa**
	Jackson Food Store
29	**US 20 / US 26 / Franklin Rd / Caldwell**
	Flying J Travel Plaza
	Sage Travel Plaza (fee charged)

Public dump station next to fairgrounds, free
> *Comments:* Turn south after exiting highway and head towards town, past the Sage Travel Plaza. Turn on 21st Ave and proceed to the railroad tracks. Turn left after crossing tracks. Dump is next to fairgrounds.

Interstate 86

Interstate 86 runs east to west for about 63 miles from I-15 in Pocatello to I-84 exit 222, east of Heyburn. Eastbound travelers should read up the chart. Westbound travelers read down the chart.

Exit(mm)	Description
61	**US 91 / Yellowstone Ave / Chubbuck**
	Big Bear Chevron (fee charged)
58	**US 30 / Tank Farm Rd**
	City Water Treatment Plant on Batiste Rd

Interstate 90

Interstate 90 runs east to west for 74 miles from the Montana state line to the Washington state line. Eastbound travelers should read up the chart. Westbound travelers read down the chart.

Exit(mm)	Description
49	**Bunker Ave / Kellogg**
	Public dump station maintained by Shoshone County. From exit go south on Bunker Ave, past high school on left; dump is ahead on right. Donations accepted. Closes for winter end of October. Latitude: 47.5426 • Longitude: -116.1357
43	**Coeur d'Alene River Rd**
	Exxon Station
15	**Sherman Ave / Coeur d'Alene**
	Big Y Truck Stop
12	**US 95 / Coeur d'Alene**
	Holiday service station, 312 W Haycraft Ave, 208-664-6878, no charge. Latitude: 47.7029 • Longitude: -116.7914
	Jifi Stop-N-Shop on Appleway Ave

5	**Spokane St / Post Falls**
	Conoco Gas Station and Convenience Store - north on Spokane St, right on Seltice Way to Conoco on north side of road
2	**Pleasant View Rd**
	Flying J Travel Plaza

Other Locations

City or Town	Description
American Falls	Selcho Oil Company at Madison St and Oregon Trail Rd
Ashton	Tourist Information Center on US 20 north of town, $5
Avery	Upper Landing Wayside, 1 mile east of town on Saint Joe River Rd
Blackfoot	An RV dump station is located next to the fire station at 209 W Idaho St
Boise	Jolley's Service on W State St at N 35th St
Boise/Garden City	On The River RV Park on N Glenwood St (ID 44), fee unknown
Boise/Garden City	Stinker Station at corner of Chinden Blvd (US 20/26) and Glenwood St across from the fairgrounds. $5 or free with fuel purchase.
Bonners Ferry	Boundary County Fairgrounds off US 2/95
Bonners Ferry	South Hill Chevron on US 2/95 (fee charged)
Buhl	Buhl Visitor Center, on US 30 at the eastern edge of town
Buhl	Oasis Stop N Go at junction of US 30 and Clear Lakes Rd
Burley	Cassia County Fairgrounds, east of town, free.
Caldwell	City Disposal Station at I-84 Business Loop and ID 19 (Simplot Blvd)
Cambridge	County Fairgrounds on US 95 (fee charged)
Cambridge	Idaho Power campgrounds along ID 71 about 30 miles north of Cambridge
Carey	Sinclair station (Castle's Corner), 19601 Queens Crown Rd, dump is in back of station, water available, no charge
Cascade	Harpo's gas station on the west side of ID 55, south end of town. The dump is located behind the gas station. Open year-round (water off in winter). Free
Challis	Land of the Yankee Fork Interpretive Center at the intersection of US 93 and ID 75, free. The dump station is along the more northern edge of the parking lot, which is large enough for big rigs.
Coeur d'Alene	County Fairgrounds on Dalton Ave north of town off US 95
Driggs	Elsie's Chevron on ID 33

Elk City	Red River Ranger Station about 1/4 mile south of the old Red River Ranger Station half-way between Elk City and Dixie. Free
Emmett	Cenex Station on N Washington (Daytime only)
Emmett	County Fairgrounds at ID 16 and S Johns Ave
Fairfield	City Park at city center
Filer	Twin Falls County Fairgrounds
Franklin	City RV rest area 1/2 mile south of town on US 91
Genesee	City Park at city center
Gooding	RV dump station maintained by the city is on 2nd Ave, 1/2 block west of Main St
Grace	Grace City Park on ID 34
Grangeville	Bear Den RV Resort at Mile Marker 239 on US-95 at Fish Hatchery Rd. $5 fee charged (great tasting well water included). Latitude: 45.9250 · Longitude: -116.1447
Grangeville	Mountain Top Quick Lube & Gas at 507 W Main St (fee charged)
Grangeville	Rae Brothers Sporting Goods at 247 E Main St (fee charged)
Hailey	City Park at ID 75 and 4th Ave. Open mid-April to mid-October
Hazelton	Hazelton City Park on ID 25 at S Howard St
Homedale	City Park on US 95 by the Snake River on the east side of town
Horseshoe Bend	Chevron station on the north side of town at the intersection of ID 55 and ID 52. Dump is near the propane tanks. $3
Idaho City	Community Center in town off Montgomery St
Island Park	Public dump station on US 20 south of town in a rest area. There is parking, picnic tables, restrooms, and a dump station with non-potable water. No charge.
Jerome	Jerome County Fairgrounds on W 4th Ave
Kamiah	BJ's Auto Repair just off US 12 in town, $4 fee
Kamiah	Kamiah Shell on US 12 at the east end of town (fee charged)
Kamiah	The Station on US 12 at the west end of town (fee charged)
Kendrick	Public dump station on ID 3 at the east edge of town near the school at the bottom of Kendrick Grade, open seasonally, free.
Ketchum	North of Ketchum, turn east to the Sawtooth NRA Visitor Center. Stay on this road past the visitor center, offices,

shops, and residences, then into a large meadow. Dump station is in the meadow, just past first dump station sign. Donation requested.

Kingston	Shoshone Base Camp on Coeur d'Alene River Rd about 28 miles north of Kingston I-90 Exit 43
Lenore	Rest Area on US 12 (free, water is also available)
Lewiston	County Fairgrounds at 13th St and Airway Ave
Lewiston	Dales Boat, Camper and Auto Sales at 615 Thain Rd
Lewiston	Flying J Travel Plaza at junction of US 12 and US 95
Lewiston	Jim Eddy's Auto Clinic at 102 Thain Rd
Lewiston	North Lewiston Dynamart on 6th Ave near junction of US 12 and ID 128
Macks Inn	On US 20 at Macks Inn there is a county sewer building with an RV dump station. It is between mile marker 193 and 194. Free
McCall	Ponderosa State Park, 208-634-2164, $4 (entrance fee). The state park is about two miles northeast of town. When entering McCall, turn east on Park St and continue as Park St becomes Thompson. Turn north on Davis Ave and follow signs to park. Dump is located across road from visitor center.
Meridian	Water Treatment Plant at W Ustick Rd and N Ten Mile Rd. Open sunup to sundown. No fee.
Montour	Montour Campground (Bureau of Reclamation public campground) 2 miles south of Highway 52 on Montour Rd. $3 fee. Potable water available.
Montpelier	City Park at junction of US 30 and US 89
Moscow	Latah County Fairgrounds north of Moscow Mall on White Ave
Moscow	Moscow U-Haul at 2320 W Pullman Rd (ID 8)
Moscow	Redinger Heating & RV at 719 N Main St (US 95)
Mountain Home	Public dump station on E 12th St S, no charge. Take I-84 Bus to E 12th St, turn north. The dump is down a block on your left. Potable water is also available.
Nampa	Wastewater Treatment Plant at 340 W Railroad St
New Plymouth	Lowell's Mini Market on US 30 (fee charged)
Oakley	City RV park at rodeo grounds south of town
Orofino	Dent Acres Campground (Corps of Engineers), 208-476-1261. Campground is 20 miles north of Orofino on Orofino-Elk River Road via Wells Bench. Open May-Nov. Latitude: 46.6272 • Longitude: -116.2200
Orofino	Dump station is 1/2 mile west of the Orofino bridge on US 12 next to the Armory building. The dump is maintained by the local Good Sam Club (donation is appreciated).

Paris	Paris City Park on US 89 at city center
Paul	Public dump station northeast of town. From town center go east .6 mile on SR-25 (look for RV dump station sign on north side of highway), go north .2 mile then west .1 mile on Idaho St. Cost is unknown. Potable water available. Latitude: 42.6078 • Longitude: -113.7722
Payette	Public dump station at 7th Ave N and US 95
Payette	Poole's General Store at 1537 1st Ave S, just west of US 95
Pierce	Public dump station northern end of town on the main street through town.
Pocatello	Bannock County Fairgrounds
Pocatello	U-Haul at 709 N 5th Ave (I-15 Business Loop)
Ponderay	Lake RV/Hi Dee Ho RV Park, 1200 Fontaine Dr, 800-763-3922, fee not known. Located off US 2 between Sandpoint and Ponderay. Latitude: 48.2968 • Longitude: -116.5464
Preston	Public dump station on W Oneida St about one mile west of town center. The dump station is on the north side of the highway. Free. Latitude: 42.0964 • Longitude: -111.8902
Rexburg	Ray Oakey Gas & Oil at 279 N 2nd E (fee charged)
Richfield	Dump station maintained by the city is on Main St, 2-1/2 blocks north of US 26/93
Rigby	Bob's Kwik Stop on Farnsworth Way (fee charged)
Riggins	Chevron Station on US 95
Rogerson	Rogerson Service on US 93
Rupert	Dump station maintained by the city is at 10th St and A St
Saint Anthony	Ray's Texaco on S Bridge St at E 3rd St
Saint Maries	Benewah County Fairgrounds at 23rd St and ID 5
Sandpoint	Bonner County Fairgrounds on Boyer Ave, no fee
Shelley	Public dump station behind Food Shop gas station on north end of town, no charge
Shoshone	Public dump station off US 93 on W "E" St in miniature park, southern end of town
Soda Springs	City of Soda Springs public dump station one block north of US 30 off Main St. Free
Soda Springs	Quick Stop at 111 N Hooper Ave (ID 34) (fee charged)
Tensed	Public dump station off US 95, across from gas station. Dump station is located next to the park on Second St, no fee but donations accepted. Closed in winter.
Twin Falls	Oasis Pump & Wash at 1135 N Blue Lakes Blvd (US 93) in northern Twin Falls
Weiser	Seventh Street Market at E 7th St and US 95
Wilder	Jackson Food Store at US 95 and ID 19

ILLINOIS

Below is a list of RV dump stations in Illinois. Listed first are those easily accessed from Interstate highways followed by those in other locations throughout the state.

Interstate 39

Interstate 39 runs north to south for about 140 miles from the Wisconsin state line to I-55 exit 164. From Rockford to the Wisconsin state line, the Interstate is also I-90. Northbound travelers should read up the chart. Southbound travelers read down the chart.

Exit(mm)	Description
	▼ I-39 and I-90 run together / follows I-90 numbering ▼
1	**US 51 / IL 75 / S Beloit**
	Flying J Travel Plaza
3	**Rockton Rd / CR 9 / to Rockton**
	Love's Travel Stop, 815-389-1923, no charge. Dump is on automobile side next to Rockton Rd.
	▲ I-39 and I-90 run together / follows I-90 numbering ▲
99	**IL 38 / Rochelle**
	Petro Stopping Center
35	**IL 17 / to Wenona**
	Shell gas station, no charge

Interstate 55

I-55 runs north to south for 295 miles from Chicago to the Missouri state line. Portions of the Interstate are shared with I-70, I-72, and I-74. Northbound travelers should read up the chart. Southbound travelers read down the chart.

Exit(mm)	Description
241	**CR 44 / N River Rd / Wilmington**
	Public campground in Des Plaines Fish & Wildlife Area
109	**CR 2 / Williamsville**
	Love's Travel Stop, no fee
82	**IL 104 / to Pawnee**
	Auburn Travel Center

52	**SR-16 / Litchfield**
	Shell gas station about 1/2 mile east of I-55 Exit 52; north side of the road next to McDonald's. Fee unknown.

Interstate 57

Interstate 57 runs north to south for 358 miles from Chicago to the Missouri state line. Portions of the Interstate are shared with I-64 and I-70. Northbound travelers should read up the chart. Southbound travelers read down the chart.

Exit(mm)	Description
283	**US 24 / Gilman**
	R&R RV Sales west of exit, 815-265-7218, $10
	▼ *I-57 and I-70 run together / follows I-57 numbering* ▼
160	**IL 33 / IL 32 / Effingham**
	Flying J Travel Plaza
	▲ *I-57 and I-70 run together / follows I-57 numbering* ▲
83	**North Ave / CR 42 / Ina**
	Love's Travel Stop, 202 North Ave, 618-437-5275

Interstate 70

I-70 runs east to west for 156 miles from the Indiana state line to the Missouri state line. Portions of the Interstate are also I-55 and I-57. Eastbound travelers should read up the chart. Westbound travelers read down the chart.

Exit(mm)	Description
	▼ *I-57 and I-70 run together / follows I-57 numbering* ▼
160	**IL 33 / IL 32 / Effingham**
	Flying J Travel Plaza
	▲ *I-57 and I-70 run together / follows I-57 numbering* ▲

Interstate 80

Interstate 80 runs east to west for 163 miles from the Indiana state line to the Iowa state line. A small segment is shared with I-94 and I-294.

Eastbound travelers should read up the chart. Westbound travelers read down the chart.

Exit(mm)	Description
130	**Larkin Ave / Joliet**
	Empress Casino and RV Park, 2300 Empress Dr, Joliet IL 60436 / 888-436-7737. Dump station is for use by RV park guests only.
77	**IL 351 / La Salle**
	Flying J Travel Plaza
75	**IL 251 / Peru**
	Tiki Truck Stop

Interstate 90

Interstate 90 runs east to west for 108 miles from the Indiana state line to the Wisconsin state line. Portions of the Interstate are also I-39, I-94, and the Northwest Tollway. Mile markers on the Northwest Tollway *decrease* from west to east, the opposite of the normal numbering system. Eastbound travelers should read up the chart. Westbound travelers read down the chart.

Exit(mm)	Description
	▼ *I-90 and NW Tollway run together / follows Tollway* ▼
26	**Randall Rd / Elgin**
	Paul Wolff Forest Preserve, $10 if not camping. From exit go south to Big Timber Rd and then west 1.5 miles to park.
36	**US 20 / to Marengo**
	TA Travel Center, 847-683-4550, free
	Comments: Unmarked dump station open to the public at rear of HDT repair shop, west side of truck parking area. Marked by a white post and a spigot.
	▲ *I-90 and NW Tollway run together / follows Tollway* ▲
	▼ *I-39 and I-90 run together / follows I-90 numbering* ▼
3	**Rockton Rd / CR 9 / to Rockton**
	Love's Travel Stop, 815-389-1923, no charge. Dump is on automobile side next to Rockton Rd.
1	**US 51 / IL 75 / S Beloit**
	Flying J Travel Plaza
	▲ *I-39 and I-90 run together / follows I-90 numbering* ▲

Interstate 94

Interstate 94 runs east to west for 77 miles from the Indiana state line to the Wisconsin state line. Portions are also I-80, I-90 and the Tri-State Tollway. Mile markers on the Tri-State Tollway *decrease* from west to east, the opposite of the usual numbering system. Eastbound travelers should read up the chart. Westbound travelers read down the chart.

Exit(mm)	Description
1	**Russell Rd**
	TA Travel Center

Interstate 270

Interstate 270 forms an open loop around Saint Louis. This portion in Illinois runs east to west from I-70/I-55 to the Missouri state line. Eastbound travelers should read up the chart. Westbound travelers read down the chart.

Exit(mm)	Description
6b	**IL 111 / Pontoon Beach / Mitchell**
	Flying J Travel Plaza, phone: 618-931-1580

Interstate 355

Interstate 355 is a 32-mile route in the Chicago area. It runs north to south between I-290 Exit 7 and I-80 Exit 140. Northbound travelers should read up the chart. Southbound travelers read down the chart.

Exit(mm)	Description
18	**Maple Ave / Downers Grove**
	Downers Grove Sanitary District, 2710 Curtiss St, no charge. From exit go east on Maple Ave, north on Walnut Ave, east on Curtiss St. Non-potable water available. Open regular business hours.

Other Locations

City or Town	Description
Addison	Water treatment plant on S Villa Ave between Lake St (US 20) and E Fullerton Ave, no charge

Arthur	Public dump station in town off IL 133 at the fairgrounds.
Cahokia	Cahokia RV Parque, $10 fee. Campground is at the intersection of IL 3 and IL 157 about two miles north of I-255 Exit 13.
Cambridge	Gibson's RV Park & Campground, 10768 E 1600 St, 309-937-2314, $5. Two dump stations, one on each side of entry road past office. Located 4 miles east of town via IL 81. Latitude: 41.3064 • Longitude: -90.1252
Decorah	Pulpit Rock Campground, Decorah IA 52101 / 563-382-9551. Cost is unknown. Two public dump stations located within city park. Park is southwest of town off US 52 at Pulpit Rock Rd. Latitude: 43.2980 • Longitude: -91.8127
East Peoria	Spindler Campground & Marina, 3701 N Main St, 309-699-5615, $3 of free if camping. Latitude: 40.7092 • Longitude: -89.5340
East Saint Louis	Casino Queen RV Park, $5. RV park is at east end of parking lot for Casino Queen on the Mississippi River. Accessible from I-55, I-64, and I-70.
Havana	Riverfront Park (city park) along N Schrader St, north of US 136, fee unknown. Campground with 12 RV/tent sites for $5 to $15.
Hillsboro	Sherwood Forest Campground (city park) on Lake Hillsboro northeast of town, $3 fee for non-campers, 217-532-5211
Island Lake	Camping World, 4450 Darrell Rd, Island Lake IL 60042 / 866-885-7621. Cost is $15.
McLeansboro	Hamilton County State Fish & Wildlife Area, 7 miles east of town
Naperville	Wastewater treatment plant at 3712 Plainfield-Naperville Rd, no fee. The site is in southern Naperville between 95th St and 104th St. Accessible from I-55 Exit 263, about 5 miles north of exit.
Salem	Marion County Fairgrounds on IL 37 south of town
Thomson	Tomson Causeway Park (Corps of Engineers), west of town on Mississippi River, $5 fee
Zion	Illinois Beach State Park, $5 fee for non-registered campers. There are two dump stations in the campground and one past the picnic areas just before the main parking lot at the beach. The campground stations are for campers but the one at the picnic area can be used by anyone.

INDIANA

Below is a list of RV dump stations in Indiana. Listed first are those easily accessed from Interstate highways followed by those in other locations throughout the state.

Interstate 64

Interstate 64 runs east to west for 124 miles from the Kentucky state line to the Illinois state line. Eastbound travelers should read up the chart. Westbound travelers read down the chart.

Exit(mm)	Description
25b	**US 41 / to Evansville**
	Flying J Travel Plaza
	Pilot Travel Center

Interstate 65

Interstate 65 runs north to south for 262 miles from US 12/20 in Gary to the Kentucky state line. Northbound travelers should read up the chart. Southbound travelers read down the chart.

Exit(mm)	Description
175	**IN 25 / Lafayette**
	Lafayette Travel Trailer Sales, 765-423-5353, $5. Located 1/2 mile west of exit.
139	**IN 39 / Lebanon**
	Flying J Travel Plaza
99	**Greenwood**
	Pilot Travel Center
95	**Whiteland Rd / CR 500 / Whiteland**
	Flying J Travel Plaza

Interstate 69

Interstate 69 runs north to south for 158 miles from the Michigan state line to I-465 exit 37 in Indianapolis. Northbound travelers should read up the chart. Southbound travelers read down the chart.

Exit(mm)	Description
126	**CR 11A**
	Auburn KOA, $10
78	**IN 5 / to Warren**
	Crazy D's
64	**IN 18 / Marion**
	Love's Travel Stop, free

Interstate 70

Interstate 70 runs east to west for 157 miles from the Ohio state line to the Illinois state line. Eastbound travelers should read up the chart. Westbound travelers read down the chart.

Exit(mm)	Description
149b	**US 35 / IN 38 / Richmond**
	Love's Travel Stop
149a	**US 35 / IN 38 / Richmond**
	Tom Raper RVs, 800-727-3778, Free. Dump station is just off Rich Rd, near the Body Shop and Trailers Division building.
123	**IN 3 / Spiceland**
	Flying J Travel Plaza

Interstate 74

Interstate 74 runs east to west for 172 miles from the Ohio state line to the Illinois state line. A portion is also shared with I-465. Eastbound travelers should read up the chart. Westbound travelers read down the chart.

Exit(mm)	Description
	▼ *I-74 and I-465 run together / follows I-465* ▼
4	**IN 37 / Harding St / Indianapolis**
	Flying J Travel Plaza, 1720 W Thompson, 317-783-5543
	▲ *I-74 and I-465 run together / follows I-465* ▲

61	N CR 275 E / Jeff Gordon Blvd / Pittsboro
	Love's Travel Stop, 780 Jeff Gordon Blvd, 317-892-2938

Interstate 80

I-80 runs east to west for 152 miles from the Ohio state line to the Illinois state line. Portions are also I-90, I-94, and the Indiana Toll Road. Eastbound travelers should read up the chart. Westbound travelers read down the chart.

Exit(mm)	Description
	▼ *I-80 and I-90 run together / follows I-90 numbering* ▼
(126)	Service Area
(90)	Service Area
(56)	Service Area
	▲ *I-80 and I-90 run together / follows I-90 numbering* ▲
	▼ *I-80 and I-94 run together* ▼
9a	**Grant St**
	Flying J Travel Plaza
	▲ *I-80 and I-94 run together* ▲

Interstate 90

I-90 runs east to west for about 157 miles from the Ohio state line to the Illinois state line. Portions are also I-80 and the Indiana Toll Road. Eastbound travelers should read up the chart. Westbound travelers read down the chart.

Exit(mm)	Description
	▼ *I-80 and I-90 run together / follows I-90 numbering* ▼
(126)	Service Area
(90)	Service Area
(56)	Service Area
	▲ *I-80 and I-90 run together / follows I-90 numbering* ▲

Interstate 94

Interstate 94 runs east to west for 46 miles from the Michigan state line to the Illinois state line. A portion is also shared with I-80. Eastbound travelers should read up the chart. Westbound travelers read down the chart.

Exit(mm)	Description
22a	**US 20 / Burns Harbor**
	Pilot Travel Center
	▼ *I-80 and I-94 run together* ▼
9a	**Grant St**
	Flying J Travel Plaza
	▲ *I-80 and I-94 run together* ▲

Interstate 465

Interstate 465 forms a 54-mile loop around Indianapolis. Exit numbering begins at US 31 and increases in a clockwise direction.

Exit(mm)	Description
	▼ *I-74 and I-465 run together / follows I-465* ▼
4	**IN 37 / Harding St / Indianapolis**
	Flying J Travel Plaza, 1720 W Thompson, 317-783-5543
	▲ *I-74 and I-465 run together / follows I-465* ▲

Other Locations

City or Town	Description
Bunker Hill	Gallahan's Citgo just south of Grissom Air Force Base on the west side of US 31. Free
Elkhart	United Wastewater Recovery Center at 1143 Oak St, $5 fee
Fairmount	Wastewater treatment plant near Main St and IN 26, no charge
Fort Wayne	Berning Trailer Sales, 5220 New Haven Ave, 260-749-9415, $1 fee. Rinse water available but no potable water. Located about 1/2 mile off US 24/30 between Fort Wayne and New Haven. From I-469 Exit 19, go west about 4 miles.

Fort Wayne	Johnny Appleseed Park & Municipal Campground off IN 930 (Coliseum Blvd) at Parnell Ave, $5 if not camping, 260-427-6720, closed in winter.
Frankfort	Frankfort Wastewater Treatment Plant, 45 W County Road 100 N, Frankfort IN 46041 / 765-659-4741. Free. Located 2 miles north of town center, east of SR-75. Latitude: 40.3004 • Longitude: -86.5072
Gas City	Gas City Park on Broadway St, contact police dept to pay $1 fee and obtain combination to the lock at the facility
Logansport	City park near High St and 17th St. From Market St (US 24) in town, go north on 17th St to High St and turn right. Free
Marion	Marion Municipal Utility on Bond Ave, open Mon-Fri 8am to 5pm, no charge, inquire with employee for procedures to follow
Nashville	Westward Ho Campground, 4557 E State Road 46, 812-988-0008, $5. Campground is about 5 miles east of town on IN 46.
Peru	Gallahan Travel Plaza at US 31 and US 24
Portland	Hickory Grove Lakes Campground, 7424 S 300 E, 260-335-2639 (mid-Apr to mid-Oct) or 260-637-3524 (off season), $10 for non-campers, water available. From Portland, travel south on US 27 seven miles to CR 800; east three miles to CR 300 E; north 1/2 mile to campground on west side of road.

IOWA

Below is a list of RV dump stations in Iowa. Listed first are those easily accessed from Interstate highways followed by those in other locations throughout the state.

Interstate 29

I-29 runs north to south for 152 miles from the South Dakota state line to the Missouri state line. A 4-mile section in Council Bluffs is also I-80. Northbound travelers should read up the chart. Southbound travelers read down the chart.

Exit(mm)	Description
(139)	Welcome Center (sb) / Rest Area (nb)
(110)	Rest Area
(80)	Rest Area (sb)
(78)	Rest Area (nb)
(38)	Rest Area
10	IA 2 / to Nebraska City
	Cross Roads Texaco
	Sapp Brothers Truck Stop

Interstate 35

Interstate 35 runs north to south for 219 miles from the Minnesota state line to the Missouri state line. Part of the Interstate is also I-80. Northbound travelers should read up the chart. Southbound travelers read down the chart.

Exit(mm)	Description
(214)	Welcome Center
(159)	Rest Area
(120)	Rest Area (nb)
(119)	Rest Area (sb)
▼ I-35 and I-80 run together / follows I-80 numbering ▼	
126	Douglas Ave / Urbandale
	Pilot Travel Center
▲ I-35 and I-80 run together / follows I-80 numbering ▲	

(32)	Rest Area
(7)	Welcome Center

Interstate 80

Interstate 80 runs east to west for 307 miles from the Illinois state line to the Nebraska state line. A portion of the Interstate is also I-35. Eastbound travelers should read up the chart. Westbound travelers read down the chart.

Exit(mm)	Description
292	**IA 130 / Northwest Blvd**
	Flying J Travel Plaza
(270)	Welcome Center (wb) / Rest Area (eb)
259	**Springdale / to West Liberty**
	Amoco Travel Plaza
(237)	Rest Area
(208)	Rest Area
(180)	Rest Area (dump station in eastbound rest area only)
(147)	Rest Area
▼ *I-35 and I-80 run together / follows I-80 numbering* ▼	
126	**Douglas Ave / Urbandale**
	Pilot Travel Center
▲ *I-35 and I-80 run together / follows I-80 numbering* ▲	
(119)	Rest Area
(81)	Rest Area (eb)
(80)	Rest Area (wb)
40	**US 59 / Avoca**
	Wings America Travel Center
23	**298th St / Neola**
	Arrowhead Park, 29357 310th St, Neola IA 51559 / 712-485-2295. Cost is unknown.
(19)	Welcome Center (eb) / Rest Area (wb)

Interstate 380

Interstate 380 is a 72-mile spur route off I-80 that connects Iowa City with Waterloo. It is a north/south route. Northbound travelers should read up the chart. Southbound travelers read down the chart.

Exit(mm)	Description
70	**River Forest Rd / Evansdale**
	Deerwood City Park north of exit and west of River Forest Rd, $1 fee
68	**Evansdale Dr**
	Flying J Travel Plaza
35	**Lewis Access Rd / Center Point**
	Center Point Travel Plaza, 696 Grain Ln, 319-849-2700, no fee. Dump station is on the truck/semi side of the property, just off to the side of the diesel islands.
(13)	Rest Area

Other Locations

City or Town	Description
Adel	Dallas County Fairgrounds on US 169, north end of town. Dump is located in campground at rear of fairgrounds. Fee unknown
Aurora	Aurora Gas & Goods at CR W45 and CR C57
Cedar Falls	Fogdall RV, 7805 Ace Pl, 800-747-0747, free. Use Exit 225 on US 20. Site is on separate service island before entering main parking area.
Clarinda	Dump site at the Clarinda Airport near S 8th St and La Perla Dr
Clinton	Riverview Park (city park) east of US 67 via 6th Ave S to 19th Ave N at river, no fee
Coon Rapids	City park on North St, west side of town, no fee. Dump is along south side of parking area near restroom, south of swimming pool. No water.
Corning	County park on Lake Icaria 3 miles north of town on IA 148
Corydon	Dump station is on the south side of IA 2 at the east edge of town, no fee
Creston	McKinley Park campground (city park) on Lakeshore Dr
Dubuque	Massey Marina Park (county park), 9400 Massey Ln, 5 miles south of town, no charge if camping, $5 fee if not

Dubuque	Miller-Riverview Park (city park), 2400 Riverview Park Rd, 563-589-4238, $2 fee if not camping. Park is located just off US 61/151. Latitude: 42.5168 • Longitude: -90.6410
Dubuque	Mud Lake Park (county park), 11000 Golf Lake Rd, 7 miles north of town, no charge if camping, $5 fee if not
Dubuque	Swiss Valley Park (county park), 13768 Swiss Valley Rd, 10 miles southwest of town, no charge if camping, $5 fee if not
Dyersville	Amoco One Stop at 630 16th Ave SE, near the intersection of US 20 and IA 136
Dyersville	New Wine Park (county park), 16001 New Wine Park Ln, 5 miles north of town, no charge if camping, $5 fee if not
Forest City	Pammel Park (city park) one block east of US 69 and "J" St, 641-585-4860, no fee, 8 dump stations
Fort Dodge	Kennedy Memorial County Park at 1415 Nelson Ave, north of town
Fort Dodge	Webster County Fairgrounds, 22770 Old Hwy 169
Fredericksburg	Public dump station in front of city garage on the west end of town, north side of US 18, no fee
Hancock	Botna Bend Park, 42926 Mahogany Rd, Hancock IA 51536 / 712-741-5465. Cost is unknown. County park located 8 miles south of I-80 Exit 40.
Hawarden	City park on 13th St one block east of IA 10 (Avenue E). Free. Fresh potable water available.
Hawarden	Oak Grove County Park about 6 miles north of town via CR K-18 (Cherry Ave). Free. Camping and fresh water also available.
Honey Creek	Hitchcock Nature Center, 27792 Ski Hill Loop, Honey Creek IA 51542 / 712-545-3283. County park is located four miles east of I-29 Exit 66. Dump fee is not known but there is an entrance fee. Camping available. Latitude: 41.4168 • Longitude: -95.8529
Keokuk	Victory Park (city park) on Mississippi Dr at Main St. Not well marked. Free
Lime Springs	Lime Springs Travel Plaza at US 63 and IA 157
Maquoketa	Horseshoe Pond (city park) on S Main St about one mile off US 61, no fee.
Marion	Squaw Creek Park (county park) at IA 100 and US 151, $3. Enter the park then make first right and another right; follow signs about 1/4 mile into park.
Marshalltown	Riverview City Park at IA 14 and Woodland St, north end of town, no fee, camping available

Muscatine	Water pollution control plant, 1202 Musser St, 563-263-2752, no charge. Located west of US Hwy 61 on Musser St.
New Albin	Rest area on IA 26, north edge of town on Minnesota border, no fee
Orange City	Veteran's Memorial Park (city park) campground on Iowa Ave SW
Perry	Pattee City Park on W 3rd St
Red Oak	Legion Park (city park) south of US 34 off IA 48 and Alix St
Sanborn	Miller Park, south of US 18 at Redwood Ave on western end of town, also has a golf course and campground
Sherrill	Finley's Landing (county park), 24500 Finley's Landing Rd, no charge if camping, $5 fee if not
Sibley	Osceola County Fairgrounds on 9th St between 1st Ave W and 2nd Ave W
Sibley	Sam Robinson Memorial Park at 700 11th Ave
Sioux Center	Co-op Gas & Oil at 153 N Main Ave (US 75)
Spencer	Leach Park campground (city park) at 305 4th St SE, free if camping, $2 if not
Spirit Lake	Vick's Corner at IA 9 and IA 86 west of Spirit Lake
Stratford	Stratford City Park two blocks north and two blocks west of Hwy 75. 31-site campground with electric hookups also available. Dump station is at southwest corner of park. Free
Tipton	Municipal dump station located on the west side of the public works building at corner of South St and Lynn St, one block west of IA 38. Rinse water available April thru October. Free
West Bend	Grotto of the Redemption campground on 1st Ave NW off IA 15
Winterset	Fairgrounds on Summit St, southwest of town
Winterset	Winterset City Park campground near 10th St and Court St
Woodbine	City park near 6th and Park St, west of US 30, small station -- older, on south side of park, narrow rresidential streets, no charge.

KANSAS

Below is a list of RV dump stations in Kansas. Listed first are those easily accessed from Interstate highways followed by those in other locations throughout the state.

Interstate 35

I-35 runs north to south for 235 miles from the Missouri state line to the Oklahoma state line. A portion of the Interstate is also the Kansas Turnpike. Northbound travelers should read up the chart. Southbound travelers read down the chart.

Exit(mm)	Description
207	**Gardner Rd / Gardner**
	Olathe Ford RV Center, 19310 S Gardner Rd, Gardner KS 66030 / 913-856-8145. $10 plus tax. Latitude: 38.7782 • Longitude: -94.9274
(175)	Rest Area
127	**US 50 / KS 57 / Newton**
	Flying J Travel Plaza, 4245 W US 50, 620-343-2717, free

Interstate 70

I-70 runs east to west for 423 miles from the Missouri state line to the Colorado state line. A segment is also the Kansas Turnpike. Eastbound travelers should read up the chart. Westbound travelers read down the chart.

Exit(mm)	Description
411b	**I-435 / Kansas City**
	Cabela's - Use I-435 Exit 13b
341	**KS 30 / Elm Rd / Maple Hill**
	Maple Hill Truck Stop
(336)	Rest Area
(310)	Rest Area
295	**US 77 / KS 18 / Marysville**
	Sapp Brothers Truck Stop
(294)	Rest Area
(265)	Rest Area
253	**Ohio St / Salina**
	Flying J Travel Plaza, 2250 Ohio St, 785-825-5300

252	**N 9th St / Salina**
	Thomas Park (city park) about 1/2 mile south of exit on west side of road. Overnight parking is permitted. Fee unknown. 785-309-5765
(224)	Rest Area
206	**KS 232 / Wilson**
	The Waterin' Hole
(187)	Rest Area
145	**Washington St / Ellis**
	Ellis Travel Plaza, 200 Washington St, Ellis KS 67637 / 785-726-2528. Free. Latitude: 38.9473 • Longitude: -99.5603
(132)	Rest Area
(97)	Rest Area
(48)	Rest Area
17	**KS 27 / Goodland**
	Mid America Camp Inn, 785-899-5431, $5 fee. If office is closed, put money through slot above night registry box. Let fall all the way in (don't leave on shelf).
(7)	Welcome Center (eb) / Rest Area (wb)

Interstate 135

Interstate 135 runs north to south for 95 miles between Salina and Wichita. Northbound travelers should read up the chart. Southbound travelers read down the chart.

Exit(mm)	Description
(68)	Rest Area
40	**Hesston**
	Sav-A-Trip
(23)	Rest Area

Interstate 435

Interstate 435 is an 83-mile loop around Kansas City. Exit numbering begins at Lackman Road in Kansas and increases in a clockwise direction.

Exit(mm)	Description
13	**US 24 / State Ave / Kansas City**
	Cabela's, 10300 Cabela Dr, Kansas City KS 66111 / 913-328-0322. Free. Latitude: 39.1205 • Longitude: -94.8155

Other Locations

City or Town	Description
Anthony	Coastal Q-Mart at 519 N LL&G Ave (KS Hwy 2)
Arkansas City	Newman Park at 1801 S Summit. Also has 8 RV spaces with electric hookups, picnic shelter, water, grills, and fishing area.
Augusta	Santa Fe Lake Park, 11367 SW Shore Dr, Augusta KS 67010 / 316-775-9926. Cost is $10 if not camping; free otherwise. From town, follow US-54/US-400 west to Santa Fe Lake Dr; north 1.6 miles to SW Shore Dr; follow to park. Latitude: 37.7031 • Longitude: -97.0527
Baxter Springs	City park one mile west of Alt US 69 and US 166
Beaumont	Rest area on north side of US-400 just east of Beaumont, Kansas. Free. Latitude: 37.6622 • Longitude: -96.5130
Beloit	City park on KS 14, south end of town, donation requested. Camping is also available with some electric hookups.
Blue Rapids	Riverside Park (city park) on US 77, camping is also available.
Burlington	Drake Park (city park), about 5 blocks east of US 75 on Cross St, north end of town, no fee. Also has campsites with hookups.
Burlington	Kelley Park (city park), one block east of US 75, southern end of town, no fee. Also has campsites with hookups.
Chanute	Santa Fe City Park south end of town near Nu-Wa RV plant, 35th St Pkwy and S Santa Fe St. Free camping for 48-hour period, $3 per night after that.
Chetopa	Dump is near city park, behind fire station on US 166, no fee. Campground with electric hookups available in city park, $5 for RVs
Coffeyville	Walter Johnson Park (city park) on the east side of town near junction of highways US 169 and US 160. Also has 72 campsites with electric hookups for $4 per night. No fee charged for use of dump station. There is also a water hose for flushing black tank. No potable water.
Concordia	Public dump station across from Wal-Mart on US-81. There is a small city-owned campground with a dump station. Donation requested. Very nice little community campground. Dump station is by the National Guard Armory. Latitude: 39.5462 • Longitude: -97.6573

Cottonwood Falls	Swope Park/Chase County Fairgrounds across from Casey's General store at Walnut St and Union St (east side of KS Hwy 177). Free. Three RV sites with electric hookups for about $5 per night. Latitude: 38.3696 • Longitude: -96.5385
Deerfield	Country Corner West at US 50 and Main St
Derby	Derby water treatment plant, 1501 S Hwy 15, about one mile south of town on west side of highway. Open Mon-Fri 9am to 5pm, 316-788-1151, free.
Garnett	North Lake Park (city park), north end of town at US 59 and Park St, no charge
Greensburg	The Big Well tourist attraction at Sycamore St and Wisconsin Ave, $3 fee (waived with purchase of two tickets)
Hill City	RV dump is at 901 W Main St (US 24)
Hillsboro	Memorial Park (city park) at D St and Ash St. From US 56, go south on Ash St for one mile to D St and go west one block. Dump station is located at the northeast corner of the restroom building. Park also has four campsites with water and electricity for $8 per night.
Horton	Dump station is on north side of US 73 at east edge of town, site is marked but not too well so be attentive, no fee
La Cygne	Lake La Cygne (Linn County Park), 23095 Valley Rd, 913-757-6633, fee unknown. Park is located east of US 69 at KS 152 exit.
Liberal	Arkalon Park, ten miles east of town on US 54, camping available
Liberal	City wastewater treatment plant on US 83 bypass
Lincoln	Public dump station is about one mile south of town on the west side of KS 14, no fee. Visitor comments: "Not much of a site but kind of a welcome place when in dire need"
Marysville	City Park on S 10th St (US 77) at the southern end of town
McPherson	A public dump station is located on the 4H fair grounds, 1/2 block south of First St between Hickory and Mulberry streets. Open early April to late September. Free.
Meade	City park on US 54 east of town, no fee, fresh water, free overnight parking
Mullinville	Sunflower Plaza at US 54 and Main St
Ottawa	Michigan Valley Park (Corp of Engineers) at Pomona Lake on north end of dam about 18 miles west of town

Parsons	Marvel Park (city park) at 10th St and Main St (US 400), 620-421-7000, free. The dump is close to the maintenance building, which houses the restrooms. Camping available for $5 per night (electric & water hookups). Latitude: 37.3392 • Longitude: -95.2460
Parsons	Stockyard Travel Plaza, 2431 N 16th, Parsons KS 67357 / 620-421-8900. Free. Located just south of the US-400 and US-59 junction, east side of US-59.
Perry	Rock Creek Campground (Corps of Engineers) on west side of Perry Lake. Free. Fresh water and flush water also available.
Perry	Slough Creek Campground (Corps of Engineers) on east side of Perry Lake. Free. Fresh water and flush water also available.
Pittsburg	Lincoln Park (city park) on US 69 Bypass at 20th St. Park also has about 8 campsites with electric and water hookups at $10 per night.
Plainville	City RV park along US 183 north of town. Campsites with concrete pads, electric, water, and sewage hookups, $3 per night.
South Hutchinson	Plaza Go at US 50 and S Main St (KS 96)
Stockton	Rooks County fairgrounds
Sublette	Stockade Travel Plaza on US 83
Topeka	Kansas Expocentre Fairgrounds on Topeka Blvd between 17th and 21st streets. Can be reached from I-70 Exit 361A and traveling south or from I-470 Exit 6 and traveling north. $2 fee.
Topeka	Shawnee Lake Park (county park) at campground on east side of lake between SE 29th St and SE 37th St via SE Croco Rd. Phone: 785-267-1156
Tribune	Ampride at KS 96 and KS 27
Ulysses	Behind City Shop on W McDowell Ave at S Main St, coin-operated
Waterville	Public dump station in city park campground. Free.
Winfield	Fairgrounds at 1105 W 9th Ave (US 160), open year-round
Winfield	Winfield City Lake (Timber Creek Lake) at 103 S City Lake Rd, 9 miles north on US 77 and 6 miles east on CR 8

KENTUCKY

Below is a list of RV dump stations in Kentucky. Listed first are those easily accessed from Interstate highways followed by those in other locations throughout the state.

Interstate 24

Interstate 24 runs east to west for 94 miles from the Tennessee state line to the Illinois state line. Eastbound travelers should read up the chart. Westbound travelers read down the chart.

Exit(mm)	Description
86	**US 41A / to Fort Campbell**
	Flying J Travel Plaza
	Pilot Travel Center

Interstate 64

Interstate 64 runs east to west for 192 miles from the West Virginia state line to the Indiana state line. Eastbound travelers should read up the chart. Westbound travelers read down the chart.

Exit(mm)	Description
185	**KY 180 / Cannonsburg**
	Flying J Travel Plaza
43	**KY 395 / Waddy**
	Flying J Travel Plaza
	Waddy '76 Travel Plaza

Interstate 65

Interstate 65 runs north to south for 138 miles from the Indiana state line to the Tennessee state line. Northbound travelers should read up the chart. Southbound travelers read down the chart.

Exit(mm)	Description
116	**KY 480 / KY 61**
	Love's Travel Stop
58	**KY 218 / Horse Cave**
	KOA campground, $3

28	**CR 446 / to US 31**
	Camping World, 725 Bluegrass Farms Rd Ste 2, Bowling Green KY 42104 / 800-635-3196. Fee for use if not a President's Club member. Available only during business hours; no wash down water during winter.
2	**US 31 / to Franklin**
	Flying J Travel Plaza

Interstate 75

Interstate 75 runs north to south for 192 miles from the Ohio state line to the Tennessee state line. A portion of it is shared with I-71. Northbound travelers should read up the chart. Southbound travelers read down the chart.

Exit(mm)	Description
171	**KY 14 / KY 16 / Walton**
	Flying J Travel Plaza
120	**Iron Works Pike**
	Kentucky Horse Park campground, 4089 Iron Works Pkwy, 800-678-8813. Four separate stations, clean with easy access.
41	**KY 80 / London**
	Tourist Information Center next to Mc'Donalds fast food restaurant, free
29	**US-25E / Corbin**
	Love's Travel Stop, 222 Highway 770, Corbin KY 40701 / 606-526-8099. Free. Latitude: 36.9774 • Longitude: -84.1162
11	**KY 92 / Williamsburg**
	Pilot Travel Center

Other Locations

City or Town	Description
Flemingsburg	Fox Valley Recreation Park (county park) 6 miles southeast of town on James Rd off KY 32
Flemingsburg	Wastewater treatment plant on E Water St (KY 32)
Florence	Anchor Storage, 8470 Dixie Hwy, Florence KY 41042 / 859-525-9525. Free for wash bay, propane, or storage customers; $5 for all others.
Lebanon	Wastewater treatment plant at 700 W Main St, open 7am to 3:30pm, see employee for help
Maysville	Maysville River Park (city park) at Main St and Kentucky St on the Ohio River, camping available

LOUISIANA

Below is a list of RV dump stations in Louisiana. Listed first are those easily accessed from Interstate highways followed by those in other locations throughout the state.

Interstate 10

Interstate 10 runs east to west for 274 miles from the Mississippi state line to the Texas state line. Eastbound travelers should read up the chart. Westbound travelers read down the chart.

Exit(mm)	Description
(270)	Slidell I-10 Rest Area and Visitor Center (westbound)
239	**Louisa St / Almonaster Blvd**
	Big Easy Travel Plaza, 5000 Old Gentilly Rd, New Orleans LA 70126 / 504-943-5000. Cost is $25. Primarily used by commercial buses.
121	**LA 3177 / east of Breaux Bridge**
	Atchafalaya Rest Area and Welcome Center
92	**LA 95 / Duson**
	Studebakers Truck Stop and Casino, 137 Frontage Rd, 337-873-9555, Free
87	**LA 35 / to Rayne**
	Frog City Travel Plaza
64	**LA 29 / to Jennings**
	Jennings Travel Center

Interstate 12

Interstate 12 in Louisiana runs east to west for 85 miles from Baton Rouge to Interstate 10 near Slidell. Eastbound travelers should read up the chart. Westbound travelers read down the chart.

Exit(mm)	Description
35	**Pumpkin Center Rd / Hammond**
	Dixie RV SuperStore, free. The dump is located on the north end of the parking lot near the large propane tanks. Camping World nearby.

22	**LA 63 / Frost Rd / Livingston**
	Lakeside RV Park, 28370 S Frost Rd, $5. RV park with sewage hookups at all sites; open to the public for dumping. Located one mile south of exit.
10	**LA 3002 / S Range Ave / Denham Springs**
	Baton Rouge KOA, 7628 Vincent Rd, Denham Springs LA 70726 / 225-664-7281. Cost is $10, which is donated to local charities. Latitude: 30.4490 • Longitude: -90.9625
	Comments: Propane tank refills available next to the dump station and the KOA is just a couple of blocks from the new Bass Pro shop! What more could you want - miniature golf? They got it, too.

Interstate 20

Interstate 20 runs east to west for 189 miles from the Mississippi state line to the Texas state line. Eastbound travelers should read up the chart. Westbound travelers read down the chart.

Exit(mm)	Description
(184)	Mound Rest Area and Visitor Center (westbound)
171	**US 65 / Tallulah**
	Love's Travel Stop
112	**Well Rd**
	Pilot Travel Center
(97)	Tremont Rest Area (westbound)
(95)	Tremont Rest Area (eastbound)
5	**US 79 / US 80 / to Greenwood**
	Kelly's Truck Terminal, 8560 Greenwood Rd, 318-938-5411, fee unknown. Latitude: 32.4455 • Longitude: -93.9502
3	**US 79 / LA 169 / Mooringsport**
	Flying J Travel Plaza, 9210 Greenwood Rd, 318-938-7744, free. Latitude: 32.4444 • Longitude: -93.9797
(2)	Greenwood Rest Area and Visitor Center (eastbound)

Interstate 49

Interstate 49 runs north to south for 206 miles from I-20 exit 17 in Shreveport to I-10 exit 103 in Lafayette. Northbound travelers should read up the chart. Southbound travelers read down the chart.

Exit(mm)	Description
138	LA 6 / to Natchitoches
	Shop-A-Lott
(34)	Grand Prairie Rest Area

Interstate 55

Interstate 55 runs north to south for 66 miles from the Mississippi state line to I-10 exit 209. Northbound travelers should read up the chart. Southbound travelers read down the chart.

Exit(mm)	Description
(65)	Kentwood Rest Area and Visitor Center (southbound)

Interstate 59

Interstate 59 in Louisiana runs north to south for 11 miles from the Mississippi state line to I-10/12 in Slidell. Northbound travelers should read up the chart. Southbound travelers read down the chart.

Exit(mm)	Description
(1)	Slidell (Pearl River) Rest Area and Visitor Center (southbound)

Other Locations

City or Town	Description
Blanchard	Polk Salad Park (city park) near the intersection of E Alexander Ave and E Daugherty Ave. No water. Free.
DeRidder	Public dump station in P.W. West Park. Dump station is in the southwest corner of the park. From US 171, proceed west on High School Dr. Go about 1/4 mile and turn right into a paved parking lot between a youth center building and a baseball complex. Not too visible from the road. No charge.

Jonesboro	Wooly's One Stop at 1799 S Hudson Ave (US 167)
Oil City	Earl G Williamson Park along LA 1 south of town on Caddo Lake. $2 fee. Camping also available.
Opelousas	South City Park, 1524 S Market St, Opelousas LA 70571 / 337-948-2560.
Patterson	City Park off US 90. Campsites with full hookups also available.
Pineville	Paradise Grocery on US 165
Saint Francisville	Green Acres Campground, 11907 LA Hwy 965, 225-635-4903, $7.
Saint Rose	Saint Rose Travel Center at 10405 US 61
Springhill	Frank Anthony City Park at 301 Church St, RV sites with full hookups
Vidalia	K Cafe at 4291 US 84
Winnsboro	Public dump station in the city park directly across from the Best Western, south end of town on LA 15/US 425. Free

Maine

Below is a list of RV dump stations in Maine. Listed first are those easily accessed from Interstate highways followed by those in other locations throughout the state.

Interstate 95

I-95 runs north to south for 305 miles from the United States/Canada border to New Hampshire. A segment is also the Maine Turnpike. Northbound travelers should read up the chart. Southbound travelers read down the chart.

Exit(mm)	Description
180	**Coldbrook Rd / to Hampden**
	Dysart's Truck Stop, 530 Coldbrook Rd, Bangor ME 04401 / 207-848-3830. $5 or free with fuel purchase. Latitude: 44.7760 • Longitude: -68.8630
42	**Payne Rd / Scarborough**
	Cabela's, 100 Cabela's Blvd, Scarborough ME 04074 / 207-883-7400. Free. Latitude: 43.6026 • Longitude: -70.3704

Other Locations

City or Town	Description
Augusta	Augusta Sanitary District wastewater treatment plant on Jackson Ave, 207-622-4633, no charge. Located just south of the Capital Building on the east side of State St. Access is via a narrow but short road towards Kennebec River. Once through the gate, turn right and then back up to the opposite direction.
Brewer	Brewer Car Wash & Gas Station, 521 Wilson St (US 1A), 207-989-5411, $7 or $5 with fuel purchase
Brunswick	Brunswick Sewer District, 207-729-0148, $6 fee, no water. From US 1 take the Cooks Corner exit and turn right (west) at traffic light. Go past Naval Air Station to Jordan Ave and turn right. Follow blue Brunswick Sewer District signs.
Liberty	Lake Saint George State Park campground on ME Hwy 3 between Augusta and Belfast, 207-589-4255, $5

Machias	Wastewater treatment plant
Millinocket	Chamber of Commerce Information Center at 1029 Central St, no fee
Newport	Valero Gas Station, 81 Elm St, Newport ME 04953. Cost is $10. Latitude: 44.8352 • Longitude: -69.2710
Presque Isle	Neil E. Michaud Campground, 164 Houlton Rd, 207-769-1951, $15
Rockland	Wastewater treatment plant, $10. From US 1 northbound in downtown Rockland (Main St), turn right at light on Tillson Ave and left at wastewater treatment plant. Dump site is a manhole cover with hole just past first gate on left (sign on fence). Open 8am-4pm weekdays; go to office to pay fee. No water available.
Rockport	Megunticook Campground By The Sea, 620 Commercial St, Rockport ME 04856 / 207-594-2428 or 800-884-2428. Cost is $10.
Waterville	Kennebec Sanitary Treatment District, 401 Water St, Waterville ME 04901 / 207-873-0611. Cost is $5. Go straight in through gate, there is a bayonet hose next to commercial ramp on your left. No water available. Open 7am-3:30pm, Mon-Fri. Latitude: 44.5280 • Longitude: -69.6529

MARYLAND

Below is a list of RV dump stations in Maryland. Listed first are those easily accessed from Interstate highways followed by those in other locations throughout the state.

Interstate 81

Interstate 81 runs north to south for 12 miles between the Pennsylvania state line and the West Virginia state line. Northbound travelers should read up the chart. Southbound travelers read down the chart.

Exit(mm)	Description
5	**Halfway Blvd**
	AC&T Fuel Center

Interstate 95

Interstate 95 runs north to south for 110 miles from the Delaware state line to the Virginia state line. A portion of it is shared with I-495. Northbound travelers should read up the chart. Southbound travelers read down the chart.

Exit(mm)	Description
100	**MD 272 / to North East**
	Flying J Travel Plaza
(37)	Rest Area
25	**US 1 / Baltimore Ave**
	Cherry Hill Park, 800-801-6449, $7. From exit, south to Cherry Hill Rd, turn right and go north one mile to park on left.

Interstate 97

Interstate 97 in Maryland runs north to south for 17 miles between I-695 in Ferndale and US 50 near Annapolis. Northbound travelers should read up the chart. Southbound travelers read down the chart.

Exit(mm)	Description
10a	**Benfield Blvd / Veterans Hwy (MD 3)**
	Washington NE KOA, 768 Cecil Ave N, $20 fee. Northbound travelers should use Exit 10.

Other Locations

City or Town	Description
Marbury	Smallwood State Park, 2750 Sweden Point Rd, Marbury MD 20658 / 301-743-7613. Cost is unknown. The state park is located southwest of town off MD-224. Latitude: 35.5556 • Longitude: -77.1747

MASSACHUSETTS

Below is a list of RV dump stations in Massachusetts. Listed first are those easily accessed from Interstate highways followed by those in other locations throughout the state.

Interstate 91

Interstate 91 in Massachusetts runs north to south for 55 miles from the Vermont state line to the Connecticut state line. Exit numbers are based on the consecutive numbering system. Northbound travelers should read up the chart. Southbound travelers read down the chart.

Exit(mm)	Description
22	**US 5 / MA 10 / West St / Northbound Exit Only** Diamond RV Centre, 188 West St, 413-247-3144, $15, closed in winter. Note: Southbound travelers use Exit 23.

Interstate 95

Interstate 95 in Massachusetts runs north to south for 90 miles from the New Hampshire state line to the Rhode Island state line. Exit numbers are based on the consecutive numbering system. Northbound travelers should read up the chart. Southbound travelers read down the chart.

Exit(mm)	Description
33a	**US 3 / Cambridge Rd / Burlington** Donahue Trailer Sales, 15 Wall St, Burlington MA 01803 / 781-272-9830. Cost is $10. From exit, east to Wall St and turn left. Latitude: 42.4862 • Longitude: -71.1873

Interstate 495

Interstate 495 in Massachusetts runs north to south for 120 miles from I-95 Exit 59 near Amesbury to I-95 and MA 25 near Wareham. Exit numbers are based on the consecutive numbering system. Northbound travelers should read up the chart. Southbound travelers read down the chart.

Exit(mm)	Description
53	**Broad St / Merrimac** Wastewater treatment plant, 50 Federal Way, 978-346-9988, $10 for residents, $25 for non-residents
44	**Merrimack St / Sutton St** Greater Lawrence Sanitary District, 240 Charles St, North Andover MA 01845 / 978-685-1612. Latitude: 42.7136 • Longitude: -71.1299

Other Locations

City or Town	Description
Agawam	Bondi's Island Treatment Plant, $1 fee. From I-91 Exit 3 in Springfield, follow Route 5 north toward West Springfield
Fairhaven	Fairhaven Dept of Public Works near US 6 and MA 240, just past the Stop & Shop.
Gloucester	Water treatment facility on MA 127 between Stage Fort Park and Annisquam Bridge, $5 fee. May be used by residents only.
Hyannis	Wastewater treatment facility on Bearses Way at Corporation Rd. From US 6 Exit 6, follow MA 132 southeast to Bearses Way. No charge.
Lowell	Public dump station at wastewater treatment facility on SR-110 just east of Bridge Street rotary. Open Mon-Fri, 8am-6pm (closed during lunch). Free. Latitude: 42.6498 • Longitude: -71.2893
Marshfield	Wastewater treatment facility, no charge
New Bedford	Wastewater Treatment Plant at Fort Rodman in New Bedford
Newburyport	Wastewater treatment plant, 157 Water St, on waterfront, small location, $5-10 fee
Salem	South Essex Sewerage Plant, 50 Fort Ave, 978-744-4550, no charge. Plant is near Winter Island Park
Scituate	Wastewater treatment facility, no charge
Taunton	Massasoit State Park, 1361 Middleboro Ave, 508-822-7405, $15 fee, park is 3 miles west of I-495 exit 5

Michigan

Below is a list of RV dump stations in Michigan. Listed first are those easily accessed from Interstate highways followed by those in other locations throughout the state.

Interstate 69

Interstate 69 runs north to south for 203 miles from Port Huron to the Indiana state line. Portions are shared with I-94 and I-96. Northbound travelers should read up the chart. Southbound travelers read down the chart.

Exit(mm)	Description
184	**MI 19 / to Emmett**
	Bisco's Truck Stop, 2989 Kinney Rd, 810-384-1344, $5, no water
155	**MI 24 / S Lapeer Rd**
	Water Tower Park (city park) at 1552 N Main St, $3 fee, 2 1/2 miles north of exit on north end of town
81	**Francis Rd / I-96 West / Grand Ledge**
	Flying J Travel Plaza, 7800 W Grand River Ave, Grand Ledge MI 48837 / 517-627-7504. Free. Latitude: 42.7872 • Longitude: -84.6777

Interstate 75

I-75 runs north to south for 395 miles from the United States/Canada border to the Ohio state line. Northbound travelers should read up the chart. Southbound travelers read down the chart.

Exit(mm)	Description
251	**Four Mile Rd**
	Charlie's Country Corner, $4
151	**E Washington Rd / MI 81 / Saginaw**
	Flying J Travel Plaza
144	**Bridgeport**
	TA Travel Center, 989-777-7650, $2 fee
136	**SH-54 / Birch Run**
	General RV, 12410 Dixie Hwy, Birch Run MI 48415 / 989-624-7000. $10 fee. Latitude: 43.2443 • Longitude: -83.7650

101	**Grange Hall Rd / to Holly**
	Yogi Bear's Jellystone Park of Holly, $10 fee. The dump station is outside the park's gate on the exit side of the drive. In winter there is a drop bax at the office door for the fee.
79	**University Dr / Pontiac**
	A&S RV Center, 2375 N Opdyke Rd, 248-373-5811, call for hours, $7
	Comments: From exit follow University Dr west .2 miles to N Opdyke Rd and turn right (north). Travel north one mile to dealership, which will be on your left.

Interstate 94

Interstate 94 runs east to west for 275 miles from Port Huron to the Indiana state line. A portion of it is shared with I-69. Eastbound travelers should read up the chart. Westbound travelers read down the chart.

Exit(mm)	Description
243	**23 Mile Rd / Mount Clemens**
	JCL RV Center, 49685 Gratiot Ave, 586-949-6400, west of exit and south on Gratiot Ave, $12
159	**MI 52 / Main St / Chelsea**
	Mobil Gas Station, 1629 S Main St, 734-475-3380, $10
112	**Partello Rd / Marshall**
	Love's Travel Stop, 18720 Partello Rd, 269-781-9203

Interstate 96

Interstate 96 is 191 miles long. It runs east to west from I-75 in Detroit to US 31 near Muskegon. A portion of it is shared with I-69 and I-275. Eastbound travelers should read up the chart. Westbound travelers read down the chart.

Exit(mm)	Description
90	**W Grand River Ave / Grand Ledge / Lansing**
	Flying J Travel Plaza, 7800 W Grand River Ave, Grand Ledge MI 48837 / 517-627-7504. Free. Latitude: 42.7872 • Longitude: -84.6777
52	**MI 50 / Alto / Lowell**
	R2C Road Service, $5 fee
	Comments: Site is two miles south of exit at 6445 Alden Nash (MI 50). Honor system if no one available.

Other Locations

City or Town	Description
Alpena	County Fairgrounds, 625 S 11th Ave, Alpena MI 49707 / 989-356-1847. Cost is $3. Public dump station is located next to the fairgrounds office. Latitude: 45.0677 • Longitude: -83.4509
Bay City	Public dump station at the fairgrounds east of town about two blocks north of MI 25, $2 fee. Use last gate. Turn around after dumping as it may be difficult to get out of fairgrounds.
Bruce Crossing	City park behind Settlers Food Store at MI 28 and US 45, $5. Campsites with water and electric hookups also available for donation.
Carson City	Public water works, 989-584-6090. Located north of MI 57 off N Division St, south of the railroad tracks and to the west about 1/4 mile. Potable water available. No charge.
Cedar River	J.W. Wells State Park along MI 35, $6 (entrance fee to park)
Center Line	Van Dyke Gas, 23823 Sherwood, Center Line MI 48015 / 586-757-8500. Hours: 7:30am-5pm Mon-Fri; 9am-1pm Sat; closed on Sunday. Cost is $10. Latitude: 42.4694 • Longitude: -83.0358
Clare	City park about one mile south of US 10 on west side of Business US 27, $5 fee
Detroit	Detroit wastewater treatment plant, 9300 W Jefferson, free
Dundee	Cabela's, 1/4 mile west of US 23 Exit 17 on MI 50, good signs to RV parking and dump, free, 734-529-4700. Closed in winter. Latitude: 41.9596 • Longitude: -83.6750
East Jordan	East Jordan Tourist Park Campground & Beach, 218 N Lake St, East Jordan MI 49727 / 231-536-2561. $5 Latitude: 45.1566 • Longitude: -85.1422
Gladwin	Gladwin City Park, 1000 W Cedar Ave, Gladwin MI 48624 / 989-426-8126. $5 Latitude: 43.9809 • Longitude: -84.4981
Harbor Beach	North Park (city park) campground at 836 N Lakeshore Rd, off MI 25 north of town
Houghton Lake	West Houghton Lake Campground, 9371 W Houghton Lake Dr, 989-422-5130, $8. On Old US 27, north of MI 55 about 1/4 mile.
Howard City	Public dump station at the city's maintenance garage, donation accepted. From US 131, go east on MI 82 about

	two miles to traffic light. Continue east another block; go south to garage on west side of street; may have to go around block to position RV for dumping.
Hudsonville	Fairgrounds at 5235 Park Ave, open daylight hours during the week, $3
Ionia	Fairgrounds west of MI 66 just north of Grand River, no charge. From I-96 Exit 67, go north on MI 66 about 7 miles. Use north entrance to fairgrounds, dump station is on north side.
Ironwood	Tourist Park (city park) on US 2, west end of town, fee unknown. The dump site is located just off the highway as you pull into the park on the left side of the road.
Jackson	Wastewater treatment plant, 2995 Lansing Ave, 517-788-4075, free. The plant is open weekdays between 8am and 4pm; no appointment necessary.
Kalamazoo	Kalamazoo County Fairgrounds, no charge. From I-94 Exit 81 (westbound travelers), follow Business Loop I-94 to Lake St and turn east. Follow Lake St to fairgrounds. Eastbound I-94 travelers use Exit 80 and go north on Sprinkle Rd to I-94 Bus; west on I-94 Bus to Lake St.
Lowell	Wastewater treatment plant at 300 Bowes Rd, south of MI 21 off Broadway St
Manton	Lake Billings Campground (city park), 231-824-3572, $3. From US 131 and Main St, go east two blocks on E Main St and then north on Park St. Open mid-April to mid-October.
Marquette	Tourist Park (city park) 1/2 mile north of Wright St on Sugar Loaf Ave. Cost is $5. 100 RV sites with hookups also available. 906-228-0465
Marshall	Calhoun County Fairgrounds (269-781-8161) at Fair St and S Marshall Ave, $5. Camping is also available. Can be accessed from I-69 Exit 36 or I-94 Exit 110.
Menominee	City park on Menominee River off US 41. Entrance road is between Angeli's Grocery Store and K-Mart. $5
Midland	Midland County Fairgrounds, 1 mile north of US-10 at Eastman Road Exit, $5 fee. Latitude: 43.6643 • Longitude: -84.2472
Mount Pleasant	Wastewater treatment plant at 1301 N Franklin St, west of MI 20 and Mission St, no fee
Muskegon	Fishermans Landing campground on Ottawa St west of US 31 Bus, $10 fee

Ontonagon	Ontonagon Township Park on Lakeshore Dr, 906-884-2930, $4
Petersburg	Monroe County KOA, 15600 Tunnicliffe Rd, 734-856-4972, $10. From US 23 take exit 9 (Summerfield Rd) southeast to Tunnicliffe Rd. Latitude: 41.8441 • Longitude: -83.6642
Sandusky	Public dump station in front of the city garage on MI 46 at the east end of town, next to auto parts store. Free
Shepherd	Public dump station maintained by the city about 3 blocks west of US 127. Free.
Sturgis	Sturgis Municipal Airport, northwest of town, free, located on entrance road to hangers, look for sign
Tawas	Tawas RV Park, 1453 Townline Rd, 989-362-0005, $5 fee, 2 miles west of US 23 on Townline Rd, southern end of town
Trenton	Marathon Gas Station at intersection of Van Horn Rd and W Jefferson Ave, just east of Chrysler engine plant, $7
Tustin	Cadillac Woods Campground, 23163 MI Hwy 115, 231-825-2012, $7 for non-campers or free if camping. Open May thru Oct. RV size limited to 35' (30' for travel trailers). Campground also offers a full service honey wagon program (they will empty your tank for $12). Campground is located on MI Hwy 115 between US 131 (Exit 176) and MI Hwy 66. Latitude: 44.1490 • Longitude: -85.3236
Wellston	Coolwater Campground, 9424 W 48 1/2 Rd (Hoxeyville Rd), 231-862-3481, $5. Campground is two miles south of MI 55 and 1.5 miles east of MI 37.
Wellston	Twin Oaks Campground & Cabins, 233 Moss Rd, 877-442-3102, $10, open all year. Located north of MI 55 on Moss Rd, 4 miles west of Hwy 37; halfway between Cadillac and Manistee. Latitude: 44.2345 • Longitude: -85.8907
Westland	Feister RV Center, 37401 Ford Rd, 734-721-2400, $5 fee. From I-275 Exit 25, go east two miles. Closed on Sundays. Latitude: 42.3239 • Longitude: -83.4086
Zeeland	Dutch Treat Campground, 10300 Gordon St, Zeeland MI 49464 / 616-772-4303. Cost is $7.

MINNESOTA

Below is a list of RV dump stations in Minnesota. Listed first are those easily accessed from Interstate highways followed by those in other locations throughout the state.

Interstate 35

Interstate 35 runs north to south for 260 miles from Duluth to the Iowa state line. I-35 splits south of Minneapolis into I-35E and I-35W. It comes together again north of Minneapolis. Northbound travelers should read up the chart. Southbound travelers read down the chart.

Exit(mm)	Description
249	**S Boundary Ave / Proctor** Holiday Gas Station, 9314 W Skyline Pkwy, 218-628-8000, free *Comments*: Lots of room for big rigs, also sells LP
214	**MN 73 / CR 137 / Moose Lake** Moose Lake City Park (218-485-4761) on Birch Ave and 3rd St about 2.5 miles northwest of exit, fee unknown. Red Fox Campground (218-485-0341) located between the AmericInn and the Conoco gas station, open May thru August, fee unknown.
183	**MN 23 / MN 48 / Fire Monument Rd / Hinckley** BP Amoco gas station west of exit about 1/2 mile, fee not known.
169	**Hillside Ave / MN 324 / Pine City** Pump N Munch, 1120 Hillside Ave
135	**CR 22 / US 61 / Wyoming** Citgo gas station west of exit, next to McDonald's. $3 fee or free with fill-up.
69	**MN 19 / to Northfield** Big Steer Travel Center, 8051 Bagley Ave, Northfield MN 55057 / 507-645-6082. Latitude: 44.4717 • Longitude: -93.2953
45	**NW 46th St / Clinton Falls** Cabela's, 3900 Cabela Dr, Owatonna MN 55060 / 507-451-4545. Free. Dump station is in parking lot; separate faucet for potable water; a lot of room and separate entrace for RVs. Latitude: 44.1350 • Longitude: -93.2494

Kwik Trip, 2270 NW 46th St, Owatonna MN 55060 / 507-446-8176. Located off I-35 Exit 45, west side of highway, four miles north of Owatonna. Dump station is west side of the store with non potable water. Latitude: 44.1388 • Longitude: -93.2529

Noble RV Inc, 3627 N County Road 45, 507-444-0004, Free. Dump station is easy to access. Dealer is on frontage road east side of interstate between exits 43 and 45. Indoor dump station also available in the winter months.

42a	**US 14 / Owatonna**
	Wastewater treatment plant at 1150 Industrial Rd about one mile east of exit off US 14, no charge, open 24 hours
11	**CR 46 / Albert Lea**
	TA Travel Center

Interstate 90

Interstate 90 runs east to west for 277 miles from the Wisconsin state line to the South Dakota state line. Eastbound travelers should read up the chart. Westbound travelers read down the chart.

Exit(mm)	Description
233	**MN 74 / Saint Charles**
	Amish Market Square
119	**US 169 / Blue Earth**
	Faribault County Fairgrounds, no fee. From exit go south to Fairgrounds Rd; turn right; go to entrance and follow signs for camping.
73	**US 71 / Jackson**
	Burger King restaurant parking lot, free
45	**MN 60 Worthington**
	Blue Line Travel Center

Interstate 94

Interstate 94 runs east to west for 259 miles from the Wisconsin state line to the North Dakota state line. A portion of it is shared with I-694. Eastbound travelers should read up the chart. Westbound travelers read down the chart.

Exit(mm)	Description
207	**MN 101 / Rogers**
	Cabela's, 20200 Rogers Dr, 763-493-8600, Free. Latitude: 45.1872 • Longitude: -93.5373
	TA Travel Center, 763-428-2277, Free. Latitude: 45.1714 • Longitude: -93.5814
171	**CR 7 / CR 75 / Saint Augusta**
	Holiday Station
	Pleasureland RV Center, 25064 20th Ave, 800-862-8603, $10. Open during business hours Mon-Sat (closed Sun).
147	**MN 238 / 8th St S / Albany**
	Holiday gas station next to car wash, free
135	**CR 13 / S 2nd Ave E / Melrose**
	Sauk River Park (city park) on N 5th Ave E (CR 13), just north of Main St
103	**MN 29 / Alexandria**
	Holiday gas station, $3 or free with fuel purchase
54	**MN 210 / Fergus Falls**
	Holiday Station one mile east of exit, free with fuel purchase, might be tight for large RVs
50	**CR 88 / CR 52**
	Interstate Fuel & Food
24	**MN 34 / Barnesville**
	Wagner City Park campground

Interstate 694

Interstate 694 in Minnesota forms a partial loop around Minneapolis/ Saint Paul. It is about 30 miles long and connects I-94 Exit 249 with I-94 near Exit 215. It primarily runs east to west. Portions of it are also shared with I-94 and I-35E. Eastbound travelers should read up the chart. Westbound travelers read down the chart.

Exit(mm)	Description
43a	**Lexington Ave N / Shoreview**
	Shoreview Exxon, free with fill-up

Other Locations

City or Town	Description
Aitkin	City park campground north of MN 210 on 4th Ave NW at Mississippi River, $3. Park has 10 sites with electric hookups.
Akeley	City park along MN 34 on the west side of town, $2. Open Memorial Day to Labor Day. Camping is also available.
Apple Valley	Lebanon Hills Regional Park (county park), 12100 Johnny Cake Ridge Rd, $8 fee. Park is east of MN 77 via CR 38 (McAndrews) to Johnny Cake Ridge Rd, then north 1.5 miles.
Babbitt	Public dump station across from the fire department on North Dr.
Battle Lake	Public dump station just off MN 78, north of the business district where the highway skirts West Battle Lake, no charge
Baudette	Howard's Conoco on Main St (MN 11)
Baudette	Outback Jax on Main St (MN 11)
Baxter	BP gas station on MN 371, just north of the road to Gull Lake Campground, free with fill-up
Belgrade	Public dump station on highway at south end of Belgrade, just behind the municipal swimming pool and park. City office is also located there. Very easy access. Fee unknown.
Bemidji	Simonson Market, 1820 Paul Bunyan Dr, 218-755-1580, free with fill-up
Bemidji	StaMart Truck Plaza at US 2 and US 71
Bigfork	Public dump station on MN 38 behind only tavern in town. Free will offering. Pay in tavern.
Bird Island	Public dump station in the southeast corner of the Bird Island Ballroom parking lot. East end of town on US-212. Fee unknown.
Blaine	Exxon Wash & Fill at MN 65 and 129th Ave, free with fillup, $5 without. Dump is located on the back side of the building. Get access key from attendant.
Bovey	City-maintained dump station on US 169 between Coleraine and Bovey, $3 fee
Brainerd	Lum Park Campground (city park) east of town just off MN 210; 18-site campground; fee unknown
Brainerd	Pine Square Conoco Gas Station on east side of town about one mile south of MN 210 on MN 25. $5 fee. Location also has propane, groceries, and food service.

Buffalo	Co-op gas station at intersection of MN 55 and 8th St NE (CR 35), $10 fee. Dump site goes into a tank that must be pumped out, hence the fee. They also sell propane. No water for rinsing. It has been broken for a year and they do not intend to fix it. It is a poorly run station in general.
Cloquet	Spafford Park (city park), Cloquet MN 55720 / 218-879-3347. Cost is $5. Park is located off MN 33, north end of town. The campground is situated along the Saint Louis River on Dunlap Island. Latitude: 46.7264 • Longitude: -92.4700
Crookston	Ampride at 1020 Old Hwy 75
Crookston	Crookston Civic Ice Arena, 220 E Robert St (US 2), two blocks from city campground
Cross Lake	Moonlite Square Conoco; north of town at intersection of CR 66 and CR 16; fee unknown
Dawson	Public dump station on US 212 at the Dawson Wayside Rest Area one block south of US 212. Free.
Deer River	Deer River Cenex Convenience Store at US 2 and MN 6
Dundee	Fury's Island County Park on East Graham Lake, 4 miles south of town
Dundee	Maka-Oicu County Park on West Graham Lake south of town
Ely	Public dump station at chamber of commerce, junction of MN 169 and MN 1 east end of town, $3
Farmington	Dakota County Fairgrounds at southwest corner of MN 3 (Chippendale Ave) and MN 50 (Ash St)
Glyndon	Public dump station behind the gas station on US 10 (left hand corner of traffic light traveling east), no charge.
Grand Marais	Grand Marais Recreation Area (municipal park), 800-998-0959, fee unknown. Park is located off MN 61 and 8th Ave W.
Grand Rapids	BP gas station at the corner of US 2 and MN 38, $5 fee. Dump site is easy to access but the fresh water hose is difficult to get to unless you have a very small RV
Grand Rapids	City dump station on River Rd about one mile east of town, fee unknown
Hastings	Public Works Dept., 1225 Progress Dr, Hastings MN 55033 / 651-480-6185.
Hill City	Sunny's gas station and convenience store at crossroads of US-169 and SR-200. No Charge. Latitude: 46.9866 • Longitude: -93.6033
Hoyt Lakes	Phillips 66 on CR 110

Hutchinson	Masonic/West River Campground (city park), Hutchinson MN 55350. Free. From junction of Hwy 15 and Hwy 7 go west on Highway 7 to Les Kouba Dr and go south. City park campground and dump station is straight ahead approximately 1000 feet. Latitude: 44.8934 • Longitude: -94.3886
Isle	Cenex gas station, 925 S Hwy 47, 320-676-3865, free. May be closed in extremely cold weather; call ahead to confirm. Easy in and out. Latitude: 46.1376 • Longitude: -93.4589
Jackson	Loon Lake area county parks, 11 miles southwest of town, west of US 71 via CR 4
Kandiyohi	Kandiyohi County Park #3 on Diamond Lake, 6920 CR 4 NE, 9 miles northeast of town via US 12 and CR 4
Lake Benton	Hole in the Mountain County Park, west of town off US Hwy 14, $3 for non-campers. Latitude: 44.2659 • Longitude: -96.3038
Lake Lillian	Kandiyohi County Park #1 on Kandiyohi Lake, 14391 45th St SE (CR 81), 3 miles east of US 71 via 150th Ave SE (CR 82)
Lake Lillian	Kandiyohi County Park #2 on Kandiyohi Lake, 9122 123rd Ave SE, 5 miles north of town via CR 8
Lakeville	Public dump station on Ipava Ave just north of 185th St next to water treatment facility. Fee unknown.
Little Falls	Holiday Stationstore, 1704 1st Ave NE, Little Falls MN 56345-3308 / 320-632-2406. Free. Holiday Stationstore is east of US 10 on MN 27. Dump is in back.
Little Falls	Zarns Oil Company at US 10 and Haven Rd (CR 76)
Lutsen	Cascade River State Park, 3481 W Hwy 61, 218-387-3053, $3
Mankato	Gag's Camper Way, 507-345-5858, $2.50. Dealer is two miles south of Mankato on US 169 and MN 60.
Mankato	Public dump station on North River Dr, free. From US 169, turn east on Webster Ave and then immediately turn right onto N River Dr. Road ends at dump station. Closed Labor Day to Memorial Day. Latitude: 44.1766 • Longitude: -94.0068
Marshall	Ampride at US 59 and MN 23
Mora	County fair grounds about two blocks north of MN 65 and S Union St intersection on south end of town, no fee.
Mounds View	Holiday Station at County Road 10 and Silver Lake Road, no fee. Site is 2 miles west of I-35W Exit 28b. County Road 10 is not the same as US 10, which is nearby.

Mountain Iron	Little Joe's Gas Station on US 69, $3 or free with fill-up. Dump station is by the car wash.
Nashwauk	City park on MN 65, north end of town
New London	Kandiyohi County Park #7 on Games Lake, 20944 CR 5 NW, 9 miles west of town via MN 9 and CR 5
New York Mills	Cenex Station (Coop Services Inc) at US 10 and CR 67, 218-385-4620, no fee
Newport	Imperial Camper Sales, 1156 Hastings Ave, 651-459-1804, $5. Dump station is at north end of building attached to service shop. Open 9am to 5pm Mon thru Fri; call on Sat to confirm if open. From I-494 Exit 63B, south on US 10/61, exit at Glen Road overpass, take left and follow to front road (Hastings Ave), take left and follow to Imperial Camper Sales. Latitude: 44.8666 • Longitude: -92.9981
Onamia	Public dump station next to visitor center by the water tower, free
Orr	Public dump station at visitor center on US-53. Cost to dump is $8. Fresh water available for $5 (25-100 gallons). Get key and pay in visitor center during operating hours (hours unknown).
Ortonville	Public dump station located on the east side of city wastewater pumping station about 2 blocks west of SR-7 on Jackson Ave. No charge.
Pelican Rapids	Public dump station in city park about 3 blocks east of US-59 on SR-108. Park is just north of the swimming pool.
Pequot Lakes	A-Pine Express on MN 371 at CR 16, two miles north of town, $3 or free with $20 purchase
Perham	Perham Oasis at US 10 and MN 78
Pipestone	Watertower Park (city park) on 2nd St NE one block west of US 75, no charge, water available
Princeton	Conoco service station at US 169 and LaGrande Ave, $5. Dump is behind the car wash.
Princeton	Public dump station in Mark Park (city park) at 4th St S and 11th Ave S. Non-potable water available. Free.
Prior Lake	Dakota Meadows RV Park & Campground (800-653-2267) next to Mystic Lake Casino, fee unknown.
Rochester	Cenex Station (Greenway Coop), 1740 3rd Ave SE, 507-288-1245. Get the "key" at the gas station. Drive up along the warehouse, dump is on the north side. Free with fuel or LP purchase. Water available. Latitude: 43.9971 • Longitude: -92.4585

Rochester	Wastewater treatment plant on 37th St (CR 22) between US 52 and US 63, north end of town, $1 fee, large concrete turnaround, unmanned and open 24/7
Rosemount	Public dump station at city garage one block east of MN 3 on 145th St and then north on Brazil Rd. Free
Sebeka	City park on US 71, $3
Silver Bay	City waste disposal station off MN 61, free. Turn west off MN 61 at lights and follow signs for overlook. Dump station open all year, though snow may be a problem. Fresh and rinse water shut off after the first freeze.
Spring Valley	Public dump station east of town on north side of MN 16. It is located just off the road on a gravel pad. The actual dump location is not well marked, there is a five-foot tall pole on either side of the site. No water. No fee. It is near the city's wastewater treatment plant.
Swan River	One Stop Travel Plaza at US 2 and MN 65
Thief River Falls	Dump is on Oakland Park Rd adjacent to Pioneer Village
Two Harbors	The Big Dog Car Pet Wash, 401 7th Ave, 218-834-0701, across from the Holiday gas station, fee not known
Tyler	Public dump station on the east side of fire department building at Tyler St and Lincoln St. Fee not known.
Walker	City park off MN 371 in downtown Walker, north side of highway, water available, no charge.
Willmar	Sunray Square Phillips 66 just north of town where US 71 and MN 23 merge, $8. They also offer overnight parking with electrical hookups in a well-lit location. Also a nice cafe and deli.
Willmar	Willmar City Sewage Plant at Willmar Ave and 7th St behind the mall. Open Mon-Sat, 7am-3pm. Free. Latitude: 45.1086 • Longitude: -95.0351
Windom	Island Park (city park) south end of town just west of US 71, no fee. Camping available (10 sites, $10 per night with electricity).
Winona	Prairie Island Campground, 1120 Prairie Island Rd, Winona MN 55987 / 507-452-4501. Cost: $5. From US Hwy 61 at Lake Winona, follow Huff St through town to Mississippi River. Follow Riverview Dr west to Prairie Island Rd and go north to the campground. Open April to October.
Worthington	Olson Park (city park) campground, 951 Crailsheim Rd, two miles from I-90 Exit 42 via MN 266 and CR 35

MISSISSIPPI

Below is a list of RV dump stations in Mississippi. Listed first are those easily accessed from Interstate highways followed by those in other locations throughout the state.

Interstate 10

Interstate 10 runs east to west for 77 miles from the Alabama state line to the Louisiana state line. Eastbound travelers should read up the chart. Westbound travelers read down the chart.

Exit(mm)	Description
(74)	Welcome Center (wb)
(63)	Rest Area
31	**Canal Rd / to Gulfport**
	Flying J Travel Plaza, 9351 Canal Rd, Gulfport MS 39503 / 228-868-2711. Free. Latitude: 30.4206 • Longitude: -89.1367
	Comments: Dump station has a padlocked cover over it. Call from the fuel pump intercom or go to the fuel counter and someone will come out to unlock it.
2	**MS 607 / Pearlington**
	Welcome Center, 228-533-5554. Latitude: 30.3122 • Longitude: -89.5947

Interstate 20

Interstate 20 runs east to west for 154 miles from the Alabama state line to the Louisiana state line. Portions are shared with I-59 and I-55. Eastbound travelers should read up the chart. Westbound travelers read down the chart.

Exit(mm)	Description
▼ *I-20 and I-59 run together / follows I-59 numbering* ▼	
(164)	Welcome Center (wb)
154	**MS 39 / Meridian**
	Conoco Super Stop, 1021 Hwy 39 N, 601-483-6647, free. The dump station is on the left side of the store at the water and air podium. Note: Eastbound travelers use Exit 154b
▲ *I-20 and I-59 run together / follows I-59 numbering* ▲	

129	**US 80 / Lost Gap**
	Spaceway Truck Stop
(90)	Rest Area (eb)
(75)	Rest Area (wb)
68	**MS 43 / Pelahatchie**
	Super Stop
47	**US 49 / Flowood**
	Flying J Travel Plaza
	Pilot Travel Center
11	**US 80 / Bovina**
	Bovina Truck Stop

Interstate 55

Interstate 55 runs north to south for 291 miles from the Tennessee state line to the Louisiana state line. A small portion is shared with I-20. Northbound travelers should read up the chart. Southbound travelers read down the chart.

Exit(mm)	Description
(279)	Welcome Center (sb)
(276)	Rest Area (nb)
(240)	Rest Area
174	**MS 35 / MS 430 / Vaiden**
	Vaiden KOA Shell
(173)	Rest Area (sb)
(163)	Rest Area (nb)
119	**MS 22**
	Love's Travel Stop
(54)	Rest Area
51	**Sylvarena Rd / to Wesson**
	County Junction Truck Stop
(3)	Welcome Center (nb)

Interstate 59

Interstate 59 runs north to south for 172 miles from the Alabama state line to the Louisiana state line. A portion of it is shared with I-20. Northbound travelers should read up the chart. Southbound travelers read down the chart.

Exit(mm)	Description
	▼ *I-20 and I-59 run together / follows I-59 numbering* ▼
(164)	Welcome Center (sb)
154	**MS 39 / Meridian**
	Conoco Super Stop, 1021 Hwy 39 N, 601-483-6647, free. The dump station is on the left side of the store at the water and air podium. Note: Northbound travelers use Exit 154b
	▲ *I-20 and I-59 run together / follows I-59 numbering* ▲
113	**MS 528 / to Heidelberg**
	JR's I-59 Truck Stop
67a	**US 49 / MS 42 / Hattiesburg**
	Hattiesburg Convention & Visitors Bureau, free
(3)	Welcome Center (nb)

Other Locations

City or Town	Description
Booneville	Adjacent to West Side City Park on Harold T. White Dr
Carthage	Bud's Place at MS 25 and MS 35
Clarksdale	Fairgrounds at 1150 Wildcat Dr, west of town off MS 322
Columbia	Shell Food Mart at 626 US 98
Hattiesburg	Multipurpose center at 962 Sullivan Dr and US 49, no fee
Lula	Delma Furniss Welcome Center near the intersection of US 49 and US 61, 662-337-2305, Free. Latitude: 34.4238 • Longitude: -90.4633
Lumberton	Little Black Creek Water Park campground, 7 miles north of town, west of US 11
Monticello	Atwood Water Park east of town on US 84, 601-587-2711
Mooreville	Woco at US 78 and MS 371
Natchez	Public dump station at visitor center on US-84, right before you cross the brige into Louisiana. Fee not known.
Olive Branch	Flying J Travel Plaza at US 78 and Bethel Road
Philadelphia	Burnside County Park 5 miles north of town on MS 15
Quitman	Archusa Water Park at 540 CR 110, east of US 45 via MS 511
Starkville	Oktibbeha County Lake Campground about eight miles west of town via US 82 and County Lake Rd, no fee
Tremont	Welcome Center on westbound US 78 just after entering the state from Alabama, about 2 to 3 miles into Mississippi, no fee
Wiggins	Flint Creek Water Park campground on MS 29, northeast of town

MISSOURI

Below is a list of RV dump stations in Missouri. Listed first are those easily accessed from Interstate highways followed by those in other locations throughout the state.

Interstate 29

Interstate 29 in Missouri runs north to south for 124 miles from the Iowa state line to I-70 in Kansas City. A small segment is also I-35. Northbound travelers should read up the chart. Southbound travelers read down the chart.

Exit(mm)	Description
44	**US 169 / Saint Joseph**
	Love's Travel Stop; dump station is located in the northwest corner of lot near fuel pump stations

Interstate 35

Interstate 35 runs north to south for 115 miles from the Iowa state line to the Kansas state line. Portions are also shared with I-29 and I-70. Northbound travelers should read up the chart. Southbound travelers read down the chart.

Exit(mm)	Description
114	**US 69 / to Lamoni**
	Walter Brothers
54	**US 36 / Cameron**
	JoneZ Travel Center, 2106 E Highway 36, Cameron MO 64429 / 816-632-6429. Cost is $8. Latitude: 39.7542 • Longitude: -94.2153

Interstate 44

Interstate 44 runs east to west for 291 miles from I-55 in Saint Louis to the Oklahoma state line. Eastbound travelers should read up the chart. Westbound travelers read down the chart.

Exit(mm)	Description
226	**MO 185 / Sullivan**
	Flying J Travel Plaza
123	**Dove Rd**
	KOA Campground, $10
11a	**US 71 / MO 249 / to Neosho**
	Flying J Travel Plaza
4	**MO 43 / to Seneca**
	Love's Travel Stop

Interstate 55

Interstate 55 runs north to south for 210 miles from the Illinois state line to the Arkansas state line. Northbound travelers should read up the chart. Southbound travelers read down the chart.

Exit(mm)	Description
174b	**US 67 / Festus**
	One Stop, 2285 US 67, $4. Dump station is about two miles southwest of exit just past Buff's RV.
99	**US 61 / Kingshighway / Cape Girardeau**
	Cape Camping & RV Park, 1900 N Kingshighway, 573-332-8888, $5. Latitude: 37.3357 • Longitude: -89.5785
58	**MO 80 / Matthews**
	Flying J Travel Plaza
19	**US 412 / MO 84 / Hayti**
	Pilot Travel Center

Interstate 57

Interstate 57 in Missouri runs north to south for 22 miles from the Illinois state line to Interstate 55 near Sikeston. Northbound travelers should read up the chart. Southbound travelers read down the chart

Exit(mm)	Description
12	**US 62 / MO 77 / Charleston**
	Flag Stop, 211 S Story St, 573-683-2583, Free. New convenience store and truck stop. Easy in and out with lots of room to move. Water available. Latitude: 36.9191 • Longitude: -89.3238

Interstate 70

Interstate 70 runs east to west from the Illinois state line to the Kansas state line. It is 252 miles long. Eastbound travelers should read up the chart. Westbound travelers read down the chart.

Exit(mm)	Description
188	**MO A / MO B / to Truxton**
	Flying J Travel Plaza
148	**US 54 / Kingdom City**
	Petro Stopping Center
101	**SH-5 / W Ashley Rd / Boonville**
	Love's Travel Stop, 2501 W Ashley Rd, Boonville MO 65233 / 660-882-5141. Cost is unknown. Latitude: 38.9337 • Longitude: -92.7780
121	**US 40 / Midway**
	Midway Auto & Truck Plaza
49	**MO 13 / to Higginsville**
	Pilot Travel Center
28	**MO H / MO F / Oak Grove**
	Kansas City East/Oak Grove KOA, 303 NE 3rd St, 816-690-6660, $6. Stop at office for directions to dump station. Water available.
	TA Travel Center, 816-690-4115
24	**US 40 / Grain Valley**
	Apple Travel Trailer Center

Other Locations

City or Town	Description
Aurora	Wastewater Treatment Plant on Highway 39 (open Mon thru Fri, 7am to 4pm, phone: 417-678-3050)
Branson	Branson Lakeside RV Park (city campground), 417-334-2915, $5 fee. The campground here has 180 full hookup sites, 30/50-amp electric, free wireless internet, and pull-thru sites. Camping fee is less than $25 per night.
Columbia	Cottonwood RV Park, 5170 N Oakland Gravel Rd, 573-474-2747, $5. From I-70 follow US 63 north 4 miles to Prathersville Rd and turn east. Go about 1/4 mile and turn south, park is about 1/2 mile south.

Dixon	Boiling Spring Campground, 18700 Cliff Rd, 573-759-7294, free, open mid-April thru mid-November. Campground is 6 miles north of I-44 Exit 163 via MO 28 and Hwy PP.
Golden	Viney Creek State Park, no fee. From Golden, go east to Highway "J" and turn north. Go about 4 miles. It is just before the entrance to state park.
Hannibal	Public dump station on north side of Warren Barret Dr just west of Admiral Coontz Armory
Hermitage	Phillips 66 station one block west of US 54 and MO 254 junction
Higginsville	Fairground Park at the park maintenance building (840 W 29th St) behind a Subway store
Lamar	Lamar City Park on the west end of the park near camping area
Macon	Macon County Fairgrounds east of US 63 on MO Hwy PP. Dump is on the north side of grounds.
Mexico	Lakeview Park. Approaching town from the south on US 54 Bus, turn left (west) on Lakeview St. Go about 4-5 blocks, turn left on Fairground St. Entrance to Lakeview Park is on the left. Dump is on the first right turn.
Neosho	City of Neosho RV Park, north of town on US 60 Bus (N College St), camping is $12 per night, dump is free and open to public
Nevada	Jump Stop at US 71 and Austin Blvd
Osceola	Osceola RV Park, $2 fee. From MO 13 follow Bus 13 to Parkview Dr and turn north.
Peculiar	Flying J Travel Plaza off US 71 at MO Hwy J exit
Rolla	Huffman Mobile Homes at 1349 E Hwy 72, phone: 573-364-4242
West Plains	West Plains Motor Speedway, 10603 US-63, West Plains MO 65775 / 870-994-7447. Free. Located 6 miles east of West Plains on US-63 then south at overnight campers entrance. Next to restrooms and showers area.

Montana

Below is a list of RV dump stations in Montana. Listed first are those easily accessed from Interstate highways followed by those in other locations throughout the state.

Interstate 15

I-15 runs north to south for 398 miles from the United States/Canada border to the Idaho state line. A portion of it is also shared with I-90. Northbound travelers should read up the chart. Southbound travelers read down the chart.

Exit(mm)	Description
339	**I-15 Bus / Main St / Conrad**
	Cenex gas station on Main St in center of town, no fee.
290	**US 89 / MT 200 / Vaughn**
	Valley Country Store at 133 US 89, no fee
280	**Central Ave W / Great Falls**
	Holiday Stationstore, 601 Northwest Bypass, free
	Comments: From exit go east to 6th St NW and then north to Northwest Bypass
278	**US 89 / Country Club Blvd / Great Falls**
	Sinclair service station on Fox Farm Rd. Free with fuel purchase. Propane also available.
	Holiday Stationstore, 1601 Fox Farm Rd, free
277	**31st St SW / Great Falls**
	Flying J Travel Plaza, 3715 31st St SW, 406-761-0052, Free. There are two dump stations. If you pull into the pumps at the right, you will be set up to dump while you fuel. Latitude: 47.4694 • Longitude: -111.3583
200	**Lincoln Rd / Helena**
	Lincoln Road RV Park about one mile west of exit, $5
193	**Cedar St / Helena**
	Kum & Go gas station at Custer Ave and N Montana Ave, no charge. From exit, go west to N Montana St; go north to Custer Ave. Dump station is entered at northwest corner of station lot.
192	**US 12 / US 287 / Helena**
	High Country Travel Plaza

164	**MT 69 / Boulder**
	Boulder City Park on Main St
	Comments: There is no charge for use of RV dump but donations are accepted. City park also has free overnight parking, water, and restrooms with flush toilets.

▼ *I-15 and I-90 run together / follows I-15 numbering* ▼

127	**US 10 / Harrison Ave / Butte**
	Town Pump (Exxon), 3700 Harrison Ave, 406-494-2434, $2. Latitude: 45.9679 • Longitude: -112.5076

▲ *I-15 and I-90 run together / follows I-15 numbering* ▲

63	**I-15 Bus Route / Dillon**
	Rocky Mountain Supply (Cenex station), 700 N Montana St, $5 or free with $10 purchase.

Interstate 90

Interstate 90 is about 552 miles long. It runs east to west from the Wyoming state line to the Idaho state line. A portion is shared with I-15. Eastbound travelers should read up the chart. Westbound travelers read down the chart.

Exit(mm)	Description
495	**MT 47 / Hardin**
	Flying J Travel Plaza
455	**Johnson Ln**
	Flying J Travel Plaza
437	**US 212**
	Pelican Truck Plaza
434	**US 212 / US 310 / Laurel**
	Cenex gas station, dump site is behind store, fee not known
306	**US 10 / N 7th Ave / Bozeman**
	Conoco Grantree Convenience Store, $3 charge, free with fill-up
298	**Jackrabbit Ln / Belgrade**
	Exxon Town Pump. Located north of I-90 on the west side (north of Albertson's grocery store). From the exit, go north on Jackrabbit Ln to Madison Ave and turn left (west). Cost is $2 or free with purchase. Large area for big rigs. Dump site is on the west side of the car wash. Latitude: 45.7731 • Longitude: -111.1862
	Rocky Mountain Supply Co, 350 Jackrabbit Ln

278	**MT 2 / Three Forks**
	Mable's Laundry
	Comments: From I-90 exit go south into town, first business on the left, Milwaukee Espresso in the front parking lot, parking in rear for RVs, $5 fee for dump station use

▼ *I-15 and I-90 run together / follows I-15 numbering* ▼

127	**US 10 / Harrison Ave / Butte**
	Town Pump (Exxon), 3700 Harrison Ave, 406-494-2434, $2. Latitude: 45.9679 • Longitude: -112.5076

▲ *I-15 and I-90 run together / follows I-15 numbering* ▲

184	**Boulder Rd / I-90 Bus Route / Deer Lodge**
	Pizza Hut
	Comments: Site is one mile from exit at 202 N Main St (I-90 Bus)
101	**US 93 / Reserve St / Missoula**
	Bretz RV & Marine, 406-541-4800, Free
	Deano's Travel Plaza
	Harvest States Cenex
96	**US 93 / MT 200W / Kalispell**
	Crossroads Travel Center
	Muralt's Travel Plaza

Interstate 94

Interstate 94 runs east to west from the North Dakota state line to I-90 near Billings. It is about 250 miles long. Eastbound travelers should read up the chart. Westbound travelers read down the chart.

Exit(mm)	Description
138	**MT 58 / Miles City**
	Cenex General Store

Other Locations

City or Town	Description
Anaconda	Thrifty Gas Station, east end of town, free. Gas station is next to Albertson grocery store. Dump is in back of station. Drinking water available on east side of building. Latitude: 46.1265 • Longitude: -112.9316
Baker	City of Baker RV Park on the western end of town, south side of US 12, just behind the Greenhouse floral shop.

	Located next to the city park. Free overnight camping and free use of the dump station and water.
Big Sandy	Rest area on US 87 at mile marker 79.3
Bigfork	Washboard Laundromat in strip mall on west side of MT 35 in center of town. Potable water. Not much room for large rigs. Fee unknown.
Butte	Town Pump at Continental Dr and Ottawa St, no charge. Latitude: 45.9898 • Longitude: -112.4868
Chester	Rest area on north side of US 2 near town, donation accepted
Colstrip	One Stop Wash & Lube, 3 Dogwood St, 406-748-2365, $3. Located across the parking lot from the Rosebud IGA
Columbia Falls	Mike's Conoco at 1645 US 2 just west of Columbia Falls
Culbertson	Bruegger Bicentennial Park (city park) two blocks south of US 2 on 4th Ave E, contributions requested. Wash water available; separate drinking water spigot available. Park also has a campground with RV and tent sites.
Eureka	Public dump station across from the museum south of town just as you are coming off the hill going north on US 93; across from the Town Pump, in the back of the parking area for the park on Riverside Ave. Free
Fairview	Sharbono Memorial Park (city park), north end of town off MT 200, no charge. Latitude: 47.8573 • Longitude: -104.0447
Fort Peck	Downstream Campground (Corps of Engineers) off US 2 via MT 117, 406-526-3224
Great Falls	Cenex service station on the southeast corner of US 87 and Smelter Ave, no charge. The dump is next to the propane tank.
Great Falls	Mountain View Co-op, 1000 Smelter Ave, free
Great Falls	Sinclair Station, 620 57th St, 406-727-5746, no charge. Dump is on the side of station, ask for key. Latitude: 47.4983 • Longitude: -111.2158
Hamilton	Black Rabbit RV Park, 2101 N 1st St, Hamilton MT 59840 / 406-363-3744. Cost is unknown. RV park is north of town off US Hwy 93. Latitude: 46.2730 • Longitude: -114.1580
Havre	Emporium Food & Fuel on US 2 at 14th Ave
Havre	Milk River Co-op on US 2 at Montana Ave
Libby	Fireman Park campground at 905 W 9th St (US 2)
Livingston	TJ's Sinclair, 204 E Park St, 406-222-9720, fee unknown. Slightly tight fit behind gas station in adjacent alley.
Malta	West Side Self Service on US 2

Moore	Eddie's Corner at US 87 and US 191
Plentywood	Public dump station on MT 5; east end of town just west of county fairgrounds entrance; washdown water provided but no drinking water; free
Scobey	Public dump station at Main St and Railroad Ave, one block north of only street light in town, east side of Main St, no fee
Seeley Lake	Clearwater Junction Rest Area at the junction of MT 200 and MT 83. Washdown water furnished, but no drinking water.
Seeley Lake	Lindy's across from the Post Office on MT 83, $3
Three Forks	Sinclair Station on Main St, $5 fee
Whitefish	Mike's Conoco at 6585 US 93

NEBRASKA

Below is a list of RV dump stations in Nebraska. Listed first are those easily accessed from Interstate highways followed by those in other locations throughout the state.

Interstate 80

Interstate 80 runs east to west for 455 miles from the Iowa state line to the Wyoming state line. Eastbound travelers should read up the chart. Westbound travelers read down the chart.

Exit(mm)	Description
432	**US 6 / NE 31 / to Gretna**
	Flying J Travel Plaza
430	**N 27th St / Lincoln**
	Leach Camper Sales, 800-289-3864, no fee. Dealer is three miles south of exit.
353	**US 81 / to York**
	Petro Stopping Center
332	**NE 14 / Aurora**
	Love's Travel Stop, free. Dump station is located on east side of pumps. Need to circle between the store and pumps to have the left side of RV next to the pit.
	Streeter Park (city park) in Aurora about 3 miles north of exit near junction of NE 14 and US 34. Small campground with 15 RV sites also available. Donation requested.
312	**US 34 / US 281 / to Grand Island**
	Bosselman Travel Center
	Rich and Sons Camper Sales, 308-384-2040, $3. Dealer is three miles north of exit.
305	**S Alda Rd / to Alda**
	TA Travel Center
190	**NE 56A / Maxwell**
	Fort McPherson Campground, 12568 S Valleyview Rd, 308-582-4320. Located on gravel road two miles south and one mile west of exit. $3 fee.

179	**NE 56G / North Platte**
	Flying J Travel Plaza
177	**US 83 / North Platte**
	Time Savers Texaco, 1220 S Dewey St, about one mile north of exit
164	**NE 56C / Hershey**
	Tomahawk Auto & Truck Plaza
126	**US 26 / NE 61 / Ogallala**
	TA Travel Center
59	**NE 17J / Sidney**
	Cabela's, 308-254-7889, free. Latitude: 41.1147 • Longitude: -102.9559

Other Locations

City or Town	Description
Beatrice	Diamond T Truck & Auto Plaza on US 77
Cambridge	Rest Area on US 6/34, east side of town on north side of road, no fee
Creighton	City park west of town center on south side of NE 59 (Main St). Free
David City	RV dump is located in the David City Park area just north of the municipal auditorium on Kansas St, east of NE 15
Fremont	Sapp Brothers Truck Stop on US 77 north of Fremont
Hastings	Adams County Fairgrounds at 947 S Baltimore Ave, just north of US 6
Holdrege	City park campground about four blocks south of US 6/34 on East Ave, south side of tracks, no fee
Humboldt	Public dump station at First St and Longbranch St, just north of city park, no charge. The city park has RV camping with hookups available for $10 per night.
Kearney	Fairgrounds at southeast corner of 39th St and Avenue N. From I-80 Exit 272, go north to 39th St and turn east to Avenue N (4 miles from exit).
Lincoln	Wagontrain State Recreation Area, two miles east of Hickman (south of Lincoln), Free. Latitude: 40.6362 • Longitude: -96.5848
McCook	Rest Area on US 6/34, east side of town on south side of road, no fee, free overnight parking
Minatare	Minatare Plaza on US 26
Mitchell	Scotts Bluff County Fairgrounds off US 26, near the west edge of Mitchell, 308-623-1828, Free

Neligh	City park on the southeast side of town along US 275, no fee. Follow road around park. Dump is well marked on east side of race track. Camping is also available for a nominal fee. Sites have electricity and water.
Norfolk	Ta Ha Zouka City Park, 2201 S 13th St (US 81), south of town
Oakland	Oakland Park (city park), 402-685-5822, southwest edge of town, donation requested. Camping is also available (6 sites with water and electricity, $5 or donation).
Ord	Bussell Park (city park) campground at N 24th St and G St, northwest side of town
Oxford	City park near the junction of US 36 and NE 46, no fee. Camping is also available.
Palmyra	Gas N Shop at US 2 and I St
Saint Paul	Bel Air Motel & RV Park, 1158 US Hwy 281, 308-754-4466, fee unknown
Saint Paul	Public dump station about four blocks north of Howard Ave, on west side of US 281, free. Watch for sign. Water also available.
Superior	Public dump station by the high school on the east side. From center of town, follow W 8th St west and turn south just past the creek. Camping available in nearby Lincoln Park.
Tecumseh	Dump station is behind power plant at 609 Clay St, 5 blocks west of NE 50, free
Tekamah	City park on "O" St east of US 75, no fee. Campsites with electric hookups also available.
Thedford	A public dump station is located at the Roadside Inn on SR-2. Phone: 308-645-2284. Cost is $10. RV parking is also available for $12.50 per night.
Vallentine	Northeast end of town near the ball fields at 7th St and Green St
Wayne City	Henry Victor Park on NE 15, south end of town, west side of highway, free
West Point	Neligh Park (city park), four blocks west of US 275 and one block south of fairgrounds, 402-372-2466, free. Camping is also available.

NEVADA

Below is a list of RV dump stations in Nevada. Listed first are those easily accessed from Interstate highways followed by those in other locations throughout the state.

Interstate 15

Interstate 15 runs north to south for 124 miles from the Arizona state line to the California state line. Northbound travelers should read up the chart. Southbound travelers read down the chart.

Exit(mm)	Description
54	**Speedway Blvd / North Las Vegas**
	Petro Stopping Center, 6595 N Hollywood Blvd, 702-632-2640, Free. Located behind Mobil station next to air/water station. Latitude: 36.2791 • Longitude: -115.0243
46	**Cheyenne Ave / Las Vegas**
	Flying J Travel Plaza
	Hallmark Truck Center
40	**W Sahara Ave / Las Vegas**
	KOA Circus Circus, $20
33	**NV 160 / Blue Diamond Rd / Las Vegas**
	Oasis Las Vegas RV Resort, 2711 W Windmill Ln, Las Vegas NV 89123 / 800-566-4707. Cost is $15. Pay fee inside the registration office. Latitude: 36.0425 • Longitude: -115.1783

Interstate 80

Interstate 80 is 411 miles long. It runs east to west from the Utah state line to the California state line. Eastbound travelers should read up the chart. Westbound travelers read down the chart.

Exit(mm)	Description
301	**NV 225 / Elko**
	Shell service station at entrance to airport, fresh water available, fee not known
(258)	Rest Area
231	**NV 305 / Battle Mountain**
	Flying J Travel Plaza

(216)	Rest Area
(187)	Rest Area
176	**US 95 / Winnemucca**
	Flying J Travel Plaza
(158)	Rest Area
105	**NV 225 / Mountain City Hwy / Elko**
	Phillips 66, 1415 Mountain City Hwy, 775-738-5008, $3 or free with fill-up
48	**NV 343 / Truck Inn Way / Fernley**
	Truck Inn, 485 Truck Inn Way, 775-575-4800, fee not known. Dump station is behind last fuel pump on west side. Latitude: 39.6190 · Longitude: -119.2177
46	**US 95A / Fernley**
	Love's Travel Stop, 775-575-2200. Common water supply; not recommended for taking on fresh water.
(42)	Rest Area (wb)
4	**Boomtown Rd / Verdi**
	Cabela's, 8650 Boomtown Rd, Verdi NV 89439 / 775-829-4100. Free. Latitude: 39.5075 · Longitude: -119.9595

Other Locations

City or Town	Description
Amargosa Valley	Fort Amargosa RV Park at US 95 and NV 373, $10. Local domestic water is available from the hydrant in the nearby highway department rest area.
Bordertown	Winners Corner on US 395 at California state line, north of Reno. The dump is inside the adjoining RV park, $7.50. Water is available at the gas station's hydrant to the right of their propane tank. Last chance to buy fuel for about 10 to 15 cents less than in California.
Ely	Rest area on US 93 north of town, free, only open in summer
Fallon	Churchill County Fairground south end of town, $2 to use dump station, $1 for water
Fallon	Fallon RV Park, 5787 Reno Hwy, 775-867-2332, $5. Dump station is behind the general store.
Henderson	Callville Bay in Lake Mead National Recreation Area about 20 miles northeast of town, no charge but there is an entrance fee

Holbrook Jct	Topaz Lodge, 1979 US Hwy 395, 775-266-3337, $5. Located about two miles south of US 395 and NV 208 junction. Dump is at yellow posts between motel and RV park.
Laughlin	Harrah's convenience store at south end of Casino Dr, $5 fee
Laughlin	Riverside Casino RV Park across from Riverside Casino at north end of Casino Dr, $2 fee
Luning	City park on US 95. Fresh water hydrant in city park/rest area; would need at least a 25-foot hose. Latitude: 38.5059 • Longitude: -118.1786
Minden	Carson Valley Inn Campground, 1627 US Hwy 395N, just north of the Carson Valley Inn Casino, 775-783-6630, $3
Minden	Silver City RV Resort, 3165 US 395, 775-267-3359 or 800-997-6393, $6. Resort is on US 395 about three miles south of Carson City and eight miles north of Minden. Rinse water and fresh water available. Latitude: 39.0685 • Longitude: -119.7793
Reno	Baldini's Sports Casino, 865 S Rock Blvd, 775-358-0116, $5
Searchlight	Cal-Nev-Ari RV Park about 10 miles south of town on US 95, 702-297-1115, $5
Tonopah	Rest Area on US 6/95 about 10 miles northwest of town on north side of road, no fee. The dump station isn't in plain view and can be tricky to find.
Yerington	Public dump station about 1/2 mile south of Alt US 95 and NV Hwy 339, east side of highway, no charge. Latitude: 38.9896 • Longitude: -119.1824
Zephyr Cove	Zephyr Cove Resort RV Park on US 50 about four miles north of Stateline. $10

NEW HAMPSHIRE

Below is a list of RV dump stations in New Hampshire. Listed first are those easily accessed from Interstate highways followed by those in other locations throughout the state.

Interstate 89

Interstate 89 in New Hampshire runs north to south for 60 miles from the Vermont state line to Interstate 93 near Concord. Northbound travelers should read up the chart. Southbound travelers read down the chart.

Exit(mm)	Description
20	**S Main St / NH 12A / West Lebanon**
	Wastewater treatment plant, 130 S Main St, 603-298-5986, $25. Site is difficult to find. Road is among paved parking lots and not readily seen. From exit go north on NH 12A to the second traffic light. Immediately after the second light, you will see Glen Road Plaza on the right and Electronic Super Store on the left. Turn left on the road on the far side of Electronic Super Store (It is between the super store and Hem's Flooring. The road looks like it's part of the parking lot). The plant is at the end of this road. Open Mon-Fri between 7am-3pm and Sat-Sun between 7am-10am. Go inside brick building to pay fee; may need to look for staff on weekends. The dump is on the left in the grass area just after you go through the gate. There is no water.

Interstate 93

Interstate 93 in New Hampshire runs north to south for 132 miles from the Vermont state line to the Massachusetts state line. Northbound travelers should read up the chart. Southbound travelers read down the chart.

Exit(mm)	Description
34c	**NH 18 / Echo Lake**
	Cannon RV Park at Echo Lake, fee unknown, 7 RV sites
32	**NH 112 / Kancamagus Hwy / Lincoln**
	Goodie's Mobil, one mile east of exit on Kancamagus Hwy, $5 fee. Dump site with available water. Also self-serve Mobil gas, self-serve

car wash and fully stocked convenience store. RV supplies and propane filling station. Open 5am to 9pm daily and to 11pm Fri & Sat.

13	**US 3 / Hall St / Concord**
	City of Concord wastewater treatment station, open Mon-Fri, 8:30 to 3:30, must sign in at main office and get a pass, free

Interstate 293

Interstate 293 in New Hampshire is 11 miles long. It forms an open loop around Manchester. Exit numbers are based on the consecutive numbering system.

Exit(mm)	Description
2	**NH 3A / Brown Ave / Manchester**
	Wastewater treatment plant, south 1/4 mile on Route 3A, first right to end, follow signs, closed weekends, no fee.

Other Locations

City or Town	Description
Allenstown	Bear Brook State Park, 157 Deerfield Rd, Allenstown NH 03461 / 603-485-9869
Belmont	Rocky Road Campground, 1540 Route 106 N, 603-267-1982, $20. Campground is two miles north of New Hampshire International Speedway.
Keene	Wastewater treatment plant on NH 32 next to the airport, no fee. Dump is accessible from 7am to 3pm weekdays. Latitude: 42.8910 • Longitude: -72.2753
Lancaster	Lancaster Kwik Stop on US 2 at the Connecticut River, $10
Merrimack	Wastewater treatment plant one mile south of Everett Turnpike Exit 10 on Daniel Webster Highway (US 3), free, no water, open 7am to 3pm daily
North Conway	Public dump station located behind Kitchen Collection at Settler's Green. Fee not known.
Rindge	Woodmore Campground, 21 Woodmore Dr, 603-899-3362, $20. Campground is open mid-May to mid-October. Latitude: 42.7788 • Longitude: -72.0243

NEW JERSEY

Below is a list of RV dump stations in New Jersey. Listed first are those easily accessed from Interstate highways followed by those in other locations throughout the state.

Interstate 195

Interstate 195 in New Jersey runs east to west for 36 miles from Trenton to the Garden State Parkway near Asbury Park. Eastbound travelers should read up the chart. Westbound travelers read down the chart.

Exit(mm)	Description
31b	**Allaire Rd / Farmingdale**
	Allaire State Park, 732-938-2371, open mid-April through October, $20 per night for camping, $5 entrance fee.
	Comments: Very wooded area. 40-foot coach is about the maximum and is tricky; any larger would be impossible.

Interstate 295

Interstate 295 primarily runs north to south for 68 miles from US 1 in Trenton to the Delaware state line. Northbound travelers should read up the chart. Southbound travelers read down the chart.

Exit(mm)	Description
(3)	Welcome Center (nb)
2c	**NJ 140 / Deepwater**
	Flying J Travel Plaza

Other Locations

City or Town	Description
Belford	Middletown Sewerage Authority, open Mon-Fri 8am to 4pm, no charge. From Garden State Pkwy Exit 117, follow NJ 36 east about 5 miles past firehouse to second place where a "Main St" crosses the highway (You'll also see the Mariner Diner ahead on left). Use jughandle to cross NJ 36. Take to Center St on right then second left is Beverly into site.

Buena	Buena Vista Campground, 775 Harding Hwy (US 40), 856-697-5555, $20
Freehold	Turkey Swamp County Park south of Freehold, no fee if camping
Hammonton	Wharton State Forest, 31 Batsto Rd, Hammonton NJ 08037 / 609-268-0444. A dump station is located in the Atsion Campground. The dump station is open from April to mid-December. Campground has 50 RV/tent sites for $20 per night.
New Lisbon	Brendan T Byrne State Forest, PO Box 215, New Lisbon NJ 08064 / 609-726-1191. Campground is open April to late October. Cost is unknown.
Wanaque	Wanaque Valley Regional Sewerage Authority, 101 Warren Hagstrom Blvd, 973-831-6658, $2. Open 7am-9pm daily. From I-287 Exit 55, go north on Ringwood Ave about two miles to Warren Hagstrom Blvd (across from reservoir) and turn right. Go about 1/4 mile to first right. Follow the road around condos to Sewerage Authority; dump is straight ahead through the gate at the small building on the left. An attendant should be around, otherwise go to the office in the building to the left.
Woodport	Mahlon Dickerson Reservation (county park). From NJ 15 near Woodport, follow Weldon Road east about four miles to park. Campground is on the left. Free use of the dump station if camping, $10 if not.

New Mexico

Below is a list of RV dump stations in New Mexico. Listed first are those easily accessed from Interstate highways followed by those in other locations throughout the state.

Interstate 10

Interstate 10 runs east to west for 164 miles from the Texas state line to the Arizona state line. Eastbound travelers should read up the chart. Westbound travelers read down the chart.

Exit(mm)	Description
139	**NM 292 / Amador Ave / Las Cruces** TA Travel Center, 505-527-7400, Free. Latitude: 32.2970 • Longitude: -106.8120
24	**E Motel Dr / Lordsburg** Flying J, 11 Old Hwy 70, Lordsburg NM 88045 / 505-542-3320. Cost is $10. Latitude: 32.3423 • Longitude: -108.6815
20	**W Motel Dr / Lordsburg** Love's Travel Stop

Interstate 25

Interstate 25 runs north to south for 462 miles from the Colorado state line to I-10 in Las Cruces. Northbound travelers should read up the chart. Southbound travelers read down the chart.

Exit(mm)	Description
252	**Hagen Rd / San Felipe Pueblo** San Felipe Pueblo Travel Center
242	**NM 44 / NM 165 / US 550 / Bernalillo** Giant gas station and convenience store, free
220	**NM 500 / Rio Bravo Blvd / Albuquerque** Giant gas station, 201 Rio Bravo Blvd, 505-877-9217, free
195	**I-25-Byp / Belen** Roadrunner Pit Stop, 51 I-25 Bypass, Belen NM 87002 / 505-864-4541. Free. Latitude: 34.6977 • Longitude: -106.7746
115	**NM 107** Santa Fe Diner & Truck Stop

75	**S Broadway St / Williamsburg / Truth or Consequences**
	Public dump station maintained by the Village of Williamsburg on Hyde Ave. From exit go east .6 mile to Hyde Ave and turn south. Dump is on west side of road. Open 24 hours.
59	**US 85 / NM 187**
	Caballo Lake State Park, 505-743-3942, $5 (park entrance fee), Latitude: 32.9071 • Longitude: -107.3116

Interstate 40

Interstate 40 is about 374 miles long. It runs east to west from the Texas state line to the Arizona state line. Eastbound travelers should read up the chart. Westbound travelers read down the chart.

Exit(mm)	Description
329	**US 54 / US 66**
	Ortega Shell Plaza
277	**US 84 / to Fort Sumner**
	Love's Travel Stop
194	**NM 41 / Moriarty**
	Phillip's 66, free
	Comments: The dump station is on the east side of Phillip's 66, no rinse hose. Site is not drive-thru, you may have to back up 10-15' to regain access to a drive out.
	Rip Griffin Travel Center
153	**98th St**
	Flying J Travel Plaza
39	**Six Mile Canyon Rd**
	Pilot Travel Center, 505-722-6655, no wash down water
(22)	Welcome Center

Other Locations

City or Town	Description
Alamogordo	Chamber of Commerce along US 54 on west side of highway midway through town. Free
Alamogordo	Timeout Travel Center at 3500 N White Sands Blvd (US 54/70)
Albuquerque	Giant Service Station on south side of Academy Rd NE between San Mateo Blvd and Bear Canyon Golf Course. Free

Artesia	Eagle Draw City Park north of US 285 and US 82 intersection in downtown Artesia, no fee.
Belen	Giant Service Station, 19384 NM 314 (I-25 Bus), no fee, accessible from either I-25 Exit 191 (3.2 miles) or Exit 195 (2.15 miles)
Carlsbad	City of Carlsbad Lift Station. Turn east on Plaza St off Canyon St (US 62/180) at bus station, go one block, cross railroad tracks to dump station on left. Circle drive allows for all size rigs. No fee.
Chama	Visitor center at US 64/84 junction, $3, fresh water spigot on side of office
Clovis	Bison RV Center, 505-762-7200, Free. Located next to Chevron station on west side, no water.
Hobbs	Harry McAdams Park on Jack Gomes Blvd (open 24 hours, $3 fee)
Hobbs	New Mexico Port of Entry on US 62 (no charge)
Los Alamos	County park east of airport on NM 502, $4 fee
Portales	Blackwater Draw Rest Area on US 70 about 7 miles northeast of town, no fee
Rio Rancho	Giant Service Station, 2101 Southern Blvd, 505-891-3833, no charge. Located on Southern Blvd at 20th St NW.
Rio Rancho	Giant Service Station, 1050 Hwy 528, 505-896-7964, no charge. Located near the intersection of NM 528 and NM 448 (Corrales Rd NW).
Silver City	Gila Hot Springs near Gila Cliff Dwellings National Monument on NM 15, 38 miles north of town, no charge
Silver City	Wastewater treatment plant about six miles southeast of town. Follow NM Hwy 90 south to Ridge Rd and follow signs. Free. Latitude: 32.7139 • Longitude: -108.2482
Texico	Allsup's at 1400 Wheeler St (US 60/70/84)

NEW YORK

Below is a list of RV dump stations in New York. Listed first are those easily accessed from Interstate highways followed by those in other locations throughout the state.

Interstate 90

Interstate 90 runs east to west for 385 miles from the Massachusetts state line to the Pennsylvania state line. Most of it is also the New York Thruway. Exit numbers are based on the consecutive numbering system. Exit numbers *decrease* from west to east, the opposite of the normal numbering system. Eastbound travelers should read up the chart. Westbound travelers read down the chart.

Exit(mm)	Description
27	**NY 30 / Amsterdam**
	Camping World/Alpin Haus RV Super Center, 1861 NY 5S, 800-826-4413, $5
41	**NY 414 / to Waterloo**
	Petro Stopping Center, 1255 Route 414, 315-220-6550, free
48a	**NY 77 / Pembroke**
	Flying J Travel Plaza
	TA Travel Center

Interstate 390

Interstate 390 is about 80 miles long. It generally runs north to south from Rochester to I-86 near Bath. Exit numbers are based on the consecutive numbering system. Northbound travelers should read up the chart. Southbound travelers read down the chart.

Exit(mm)	Description
5	**NY 36 / Dansville**
	TA Travel Center

Other Locations

City or Town	Description
Albany	Wastewater treatment plant, 1 Canal Rd, no water, free. Can be accessed from I-787 Exit 6.
Avon	Municipal waste treatment plant off US 20, west of roundabout in center of town at bottom of hill and before river, dump site is a manhole cover with handle, contributions accepted
Catskill	Brookside Campground, 4952 Route 32, 800-390-4412, $20. From I-87 Exit 20, go north about 9 miles on NY Route 32.
Ellenburg Depot	Blue Haven Campground, 5253 US Hwy 11, 518-594-3873, fee not known
Elmira	Wastewater treatment plant, 600 Milton St, 607-732-5115, Free. Open 8am to 4:30pm Mon thru Fri. From Southern Tier Expy, take Exit 56 and follow either Water St or Church St west to Madison Ave and turn left (south). Take first left over river (Maple Ave) and follow to Milton St; turn left (east) to plant.
Elmira Heights	Public dump station in the fairgrounds at Grand Central Ave and Fairview Rd, Free. From NY 17, follow Grand Central Ave south to Fairview Rd and turn left (east). After entering the fairgrounds, turn right; dump station is on your left.
Hawthorne	Westchester County public dump station just off NY 9A at intersection with NY 141, easy drive through, no fee. This is a county dump station located on the north side of NY 100 between Brighton Ave and Bradhurst Ave, across from the Mobil gas station. Hours: 9am-5pm Mon-Fri; 9am-1pm Sat. Latitude: 41.1077 • Longitude: -73.8027
Johnstown	Wastewater treatment plant on Union Ave, $2. From I-90 Exit 28 follow NY 30A north 4 miles to Union Ave and turn west. Follow Union Ave about one mile to plant. From NY 30A, Union Ave goes down and around a sharp bend and crosses a narrow bridge. Open 8am to 3pm weekdays.
Le Roy	Frost Ridge Campground, 8101 Conlon Rd, Le Roy NY 14482 / 585-768-4883. Guests dump free; $16 for non-campers ($12 with coupon available online).

Long Lake	Lake Eaton Campground (public), HC01 Route 30, Long Lake NY 12847 / 518-624-2641. Free. State-managed campground on Lake Eaton. Non-potable water available. Latitude: 43.9867 • Longitude: -74.4564
Old Bethpage	Battle Row Campground (county park) on Claremont Rd, 516-572-8690 $5 fee for non-campers. From Long Island Expy, take the Round Swamp Rd exit and follow south to Sweethollow Rd and turn left. Follow this road to Claremont Rd and turn right. Campground is closed Nov thru Mar.
Palmyra	Palmyra waste plant on NY 31 between fire station and supermarket, no fee is charged
Plattsburgh	Momot Trailer Sales, 240 Tom Miller Rd, Plattsburgh NY 12901 / 518-563-1983. Cost is unknown. From I-87 Exit 37 turn right (east) on SH-3 and then left (north) on Smithfield Blvd; follow to Tom Miller Rd and turn left. Latitude: 44.7059 • -73.4994
Rome	Erie Canal Village on the west side of town just south of the NY 69 and NY 46 intersection at the end of the Erie Canal Village parking lot. Free
Saugerties	Saugerties/Woodstock KOA, 882 Route 212, Saugerties NY 12477 / 845-246-4089. Cost is $20. From I-87/New York Thruway Exit 20, follow NY Route 212 west about 2.5 miles.
Schenectady	City wastewater treatment plant on Anthony St. From I-890 take the General Electric plant ext and follow signs for Erie Blvd. Follow for about one mile and turn right onto Maxon Rd Extension. Follow to Van Vranken Ave and bare left. Anthony St is the next left turn. Treatment plant is at end of street. If you find the gate closed it is okay to open and drive in, just close the gate again.
Village of Webster	Wastewater treatment plant at 613 Webster Rd. The charge for using the facility is $5 payable at the Village of Webster offices at 28 W Main St. After you have paid the fee, you will be given a receipt to hand off to the treatment plant. Don't forget to stop at the Village offices first.
Youngstown	Niagara Falls North KOA, 1250 Pletcher Rd, 716-754-8013, fee unknown, open mid-April to mid-October

NORTH CAROLINA

Below is a list of RV dump stations in North Carolina. Listed first are those easily accessed from Interstate highways followed by those in other locations throughout the state.

Interstate 40

Interstate 40 runs east to west for 420 miles from Wilmington to the Tennessee state line. Part of it is also I-85. Eastbound travelers should read up the chart. Westbound travelers read down the chart.

Exit(mm)	Description
306	**US 70 / Garner**
	Hawley's Camping Center, 4904 TV Tower Rd, 919-772-3155 or 877-883-2267, $25. Westbound travelers use Exit 306b
208	**NC 1850 / Sandy Ridge Rd / Colfax**
	Colfax RV Outlet, 8615 Triad Dr, 800-849-1878, $10. Latitude: 36.0944 • Longitude: -79.9954
	▼ *I-40 and I-85 run together / follows I-85 numbering* ▼
150	**Jimmie Kerr Rd / Haw River**
	Flying J Travel Plaza, 1043 Jimmie Kerr Rd, 336-578-2427, Free. Latitude: 36.0713 • Longitude: -79.3530
	Comments: Dump station is on the right entering the Travel Plaza. You must travel behind the gas island (clockwise) in front of the store and enter the dump station from the left for a driver's side utility area.
	▲ *I-40 and I-85 run together / follows I-85 numbering* ▲

Interstate 77

Interstate 77 in North Carolina runs north to south for 105 miles from the Virginia state line to the South Carolina state line. Northbound travelers should read up the chart. Southbound travelers read down the chart.

Exit(mm)	Description
49a	**US 70 / Statesville**
	Camping World, 1220 Morland Dr, 704-883-8078 or 888-224-3059, free

Interstate 85

Interstate 85 runs north to south for 234 miles from the Virginia state line to the South Carolina state line. Part of it is shared with I-40. Northbound travelers should read up the chart. Southbound travelers read down the chart.

Exit(mm)	Description
	▼ *I-40 and I-85 run together / follows I-85 numbering* ▼
150	**Jimmie Kerr Rd / Haw River**
	Flying J Travel Plaza, 1043 Jimmie Kerr Rd, 336-578-2427, Free.
	Latitude: 36.0713 • Longitude: -79.3530
	Comments: Dump station is on the right entering the Travel Plaza. You must travel behind the gas island (clockwise) in front of the store and enter the dump station from the left for a driver's side utility area.
	▲ *I-40 and I-85 run together / follows I-85 numbering* ▲
49	**Speedway Blvd / near Concord**
	Fleetwood Camping Resort, within sight of Lowe's Motor Speedway, 704-455-4445, $5

Interstate 95

Interstate 95 is 182 miles long. It runs north to south from the Virginia state line to the South Carolina state line. Northbound travelers should read up the chart. Southbound travelers read down the chart.

Exit(mm)	Description
106	**Princeton-Kenly Rd / Kenly**
	Flying J Travel Plaza, 1800 Princeton-Kenly Rd, 919-284-4548, $10.
	Latitude: 35.5744 • Longitude: -78.1466
	TA Travel Center, 919-284-5121. Latitude: 35.6077 • Longitude: -78.1382
75	**Jonesboro Rd / Dunn**
	Sadler Travel Plaza, 75 Sadler Rd (NC Hwy 1835), 910-892-0106. From exit, go west to access road and then north.
1	**US 301**
	Porky's Truck Stop, 843-784-2384
	Comments: This truck stop is actually in South Carolina at the North Carolina state line.

Interstate 440

Interstate 440 in North Carolina is a 16-mile route around Raleigh. Exit numbering begins at Jones Franklin Rd and increases in a clockwise direction.

Exit(mm)	Description
13b	**US 64 / US 264 / New Bern Ave / Raleigh**
	Bill Plemmons RV, 4208 New Bern Ave, Raleigh NC 27610 / 919-231-8710. Cost is $15.00. Dump station is behind the dealership.

Other Locations

City or Town	Description
Brevard	Davidson River Campground (Pisgah National Forest), $3 fee, on US 276 about 4 miles north of town
Buxton	Cape Hatteras National Seashore campground. Go 1/2 mile past the parking lot for the lighthouse toward the campground. The dump station is on the left.
Elizabeth City	Quality Inn at 522 S Hughes Blvd (US 17)
Greenville	Bradford Creek Coach and RV Center, 2773 Sunny Side Rd, 252-752-8886, $10.
Harrisburg	Politis Texaco at 4025 NC Hwy 49
Manteo	Oregon Inlet Fishing Center, 800-272-5199, free. Located 8 miles south of Whalebone Junction on NC 12 at the north end of the Oregon Inlet Bridge in Cape Hatteras National Seashore. Upon entering Oregon Inlet Fishing Center, take the first left to the parking area. The dump station will be located on the left.
Manteo	Rest area/welcome center on US 64 just before entering the Outer Banks, free. When eastbound on US 64 this Rest Area/Welcome Center is on the right immediately after the US 64 bridge ends and you are on the ground on Roanoke Island. When in the Rest Area, keep to the right and the dump station is at the end of the property, on the left next to a shed.
New Bern	Flanners Beach/Neuse River Campground in Croatan National Forest about ten miles south of town off US 70, $5

Rocky Point	Rocky Point Campground & Shooters World at 14565 Ashton Rd, $5 fee. Campground is 7 miles northwest of I-40 Exit 408 via US 117 and Ashton Rd.
Rodanthe	Cape Hatteras KOA, Route 12, Rodanthe NC 27968 / 252-987-2307. $15 fee.
Rural Hall	Bill Plemmons RV World, 6725 University Pkwy, Rural Hall NC 27045 / 800-732-0507. Cost is $15. Dealer is located about three miles north of US 52 Exit 115.
Salisbury	Dan Nicholas Park, 6800 Bringle Ferry Rd, Salisbury NC 28146 / 866-767-2757. Non-camper fee is $8 for use of dump station. This park is a county campground with 80 sites; camping fee is $19 to $24 per night.
Wilmington	Wilmington KOA Campground, 7415 Market St, Wilmington NC 28411 / 910-686-7705. Cost is $10. Latitude: 34.2777 • Longitude: -77.8143

NORTH DAKOTA

Below is a list of RV dump stations in North Dakota. Listed first are those easily accessed from Interstate highways followed by those in other locations throughout the state.

Interstate 29

I-29 runs north to south for 218 miles from the United States/Canada border to the South Dakota state line. Northbound travelers should read up the chart. Southbound travelers read down the chart.

Exit(mm)	Description
141	**US 2 / Gateway Dr / Grand Forks**
	E-Z Stop Truck Stop, no fee
	StaMart Travel Plaza
138	**32nd Ave / Grand Forks**
	Big Sioux Travel Plaza
66	**12th Ave N / Fargo**
	StaMart Travel Center at 3500 12th Ave N, no fee, easy access
62	**32nd Ave / Fargo**
	Flying J Travel Plaza

Interstate 94

Interstate 94 runs east to west for 352 miles from the Minnesota state line to the Montana state line. Eastbound travelers should read up the chart. Westbound travelers read down the chart.

Exit(mm)	Description
348	**45th St / Fargo**
	Petro Stopping Center
331	**155 1/2 Ave / Casselton**
	Governors Inn, 2050 Governors Dr, Casselton ND 58012 / 701-347-4524. Fee not known. Latitude: 46.8767 • Longitude: -97.2133
157	**Divide Ave / Tyler Pkwy / Bismarck**
	Cenex station south of exit. Dump station is next to car wash across from Miracle Mart supermarket. Propane is also available. Free. Latitude: 46.8247 • Longitude: -100.8108

Conoco/MVP north of exit. Dump station is on the south side of the building. Free. Latitude: 46.8299 • Longitude: -100.8175

147	**ND 25 / Mandan**
	Freeway 147 Truck Stop
61	**ND 22 / Dickinson**
	The General Store

Other Locations

City or Town	Description
Devil's Lake	Cenex C-Store at US 2 and ND 19
Harvey	West Side Park, PO Box 21, Harvey ND 58341 / 701-324-2628. Free/Donation. City park campground along SH-3, off US-52.
Hazen	Car wash along ND 200, east side of town, no fee
McClusky	McClusky City Park, McClusky ND 58463 / 701-363-2345 (City Hall). Free. City park is located five blocks south of SH-200 and one block west of Main St. Latitude: 47.4806 • Longitude: -100.4442
Minot	Behm's Truck Stop at 3800 US 2/52, free
Minot	Corner Express Amoco, 3630 S Broadway (US 83), free
Minot	Dawn to Dusk Amoco, 7141 E Burdick Expy, free
Minot	Econo Stop at US 2/52 Bypass and US 83, free
Minot	North Central Service Heating & Cooling, 515 31st Ave SW, free
Munich	Public dump station in the city park, south edge of town. A few campsites are also available.
Rugby	Cenex Truck Plaza near junction of ND 3 and US 2
Rugby	Hi-Way MVP Station at 209 US 2
Stanley	City park on Main St about 3/4 mile north of US 2, just north of the railroad overpass. Camping is also available for free up to 4 days or a donation.
Tioga	City park at 4th St and Gilbertson NE
Valley City	City park campground at 600 E Main St (I-94 Bus), free if camping, accessible from I-94 Exit 290 (2 miles), Exit 292 (1.7 miles), Exit 294 (1.6 miles)
Velva	Cenex Station right off US 52 in town - open during summer travel season
Williston	OK Conoco North on US 2/85

OHIO

Below is a list of RV dump stations in Ohio. Listed first are those easily accessed from Interstate highways followed by those in other locations throughout the state.

Interstate 70

Interstate 70 runs east to west for 226 miles from the West Virginia state line to the Indiana state line. Eastbound travelers should read up the chart. Westbound travelers read down the chart.

Exit(mm)	Description
160	**OH 797 / Airport**
	Love's Travel Stop
122	**OH 158 / Kirkersville**
	Flying J Travel Plaza
59	**OH 41 / Springfield**
	Clark County Fairgrounds, 4401 S Charleston Pike, 937-323-3090, Fee unknown

Interstate 71

Interstate 71 runs north to south for 248 miles from I-90 in Cleveland to the Kentucky state line. Northbound travelers should read up the chart. Southbound travelers read down the chart.

Exit(mm)	Description
218	**OH 18 / Medina Rd / Medina**
	Avalon RV Center, 1604 Medina Rd, Medina OH 44256, 800-860-7728, Free
	Comments: Family owned and operated since 1968. Large selection of RVs, Boats, Parts & Accessories. RVIA certified technicians and 20 service bays. A proud REDEX dealer.
204	**OH 83 / Avon Lake Rd / Burbank / to Lodi**
	Love's Travel Stop, 10145 Avon Lake Rd, 330-624-1000, Free. Very tight for maneuvering. Latitude: 40.9957 • Longitude: -81.9963
131	**US 36 / OH 37**
	Flying J Travel Plaza

Exit(mm)	Description
69	**OH 41 / OH 734 / Jeffersonville**
	Flying J Travel Plaza
65	**US 35 / Octa / south of Jeffersonville**
	Love's Travel Stop, 13023 US 35, 740-948-2342, west of exit.
	Latitude: 39.6228 • Longitude: -83.6150

Interstate 75

Interstate 75 runs north to south for 211 miles from the Michigan state line to the Kentucky state line. Northbound travelers should read up the chart. Southbound travelers read down the chart.

Exit(mm)	Description
135	**OH 696 / Beaverdam / to US 30**
	Flying J Travel Plaza
	Pilot Travel Center
47	**Dixie Hwy / Moraine**
	Montgomery County Septage Receiving Facility, 4257 Dryden Rd, Moraine OH 45439 / 937-224-8826. Open Mon-Fri, 6am-6pm. $5 fee. Southbound travelers use I-75 Exit 50A.

Interstate 76

Interstate 76 runs east to west for 82 miles from the Pennsylvania state line to I-71 south of Medina. Part of it is also the Ohio Turnpike. Eastbound travelers should read up the chart. Westbound travelers read down the chart.

Exit(mm)	Description
1	**I-71 / US 224**
	TA Travel Center

Interstate 80

I-80 runs east to west for 237 miles from the Pennsylvania state line to the Indiana state line. Portions are also I-90 and the Ohio Turnpike. Eastbound travelers should read up the chart. Westbound travelers read down the chart.

Exit(mm)	Description
234	**US 62 / OH 7 / N Main St / Hubbard**
	Flying J Travel Plaza
223	**OH 46 / to Niles**
	TA Travel Center
(197)	Rest Area
187	**SR-14 / I-480 / Streetsboro**
	All Seasons RV, 9043 State Route 14, Streetsboro OH 44241 / 800-948-2100. Cost is $5. Dump station is located in the back southwest corner of dealership. Open Mon-Sat, 9am-5pm; closed Sun. Latitude: 41.2362 • Longitude: -81.3361
180	**OH 8**
	Kamper City, 5549 Akron-Cleveland Rd, 330-650-1491, $10
	Comments: From exit, follow OH 8 south to OH 303/Akron-Cleveland Rd exit. Continue straight through the light about one mile. Kamper City is on the left.
	▼ *I-80 and I-90 run together* ▼
(139)	Rest Area
(77)	Rest Area
34	**OH 108 / to Wauseon**
	Fulton County Fairgrounds, $7 fee. Dump station is in the southwest part of fairground. Pay the care takers at the mobile home in park. Overnight camping is also available for $15 per night.
(21)	Rest Area (wb)
	▲ *I-80 and I-90 run together* ▲

Interstate 90

Interstate 90 runs east to west for 245 miles from the Pennsylvania state line to the Indiana state line. Part of it is also I-80 and the Ohio Turnpike. Eastbound travelers should read up the chart. Westbound travelers read down the chart.

Exit(mm)	Description
223	**OH 45 / to Ashtabula**
	Flying J Travel Plaza
	▼ *I-80 and I-90 run together* ▼
(139)	Rest Area
(77)	Rest Area
34	**OH 108 / to Wauseon**
	Fulton County Fairgrounds, $7 fee. Dump station is in the southwest part of fairground. Pay the care takers at the mobile home in park. Overnight camping is also available for $15 per night.
(21)	Rest Area (wb)
	▲ *I-80 and I-90 run together* ▲

Interstate 280

Interstate 280 is 12 miles long. It connects I-80/90 with I-75 in Toledo.

Exit(mm)	Description
1b	**Bahnsen Dr**
	Flying J Travel Plaza

Other Locations

City or Town	Description
Akron	Portage Lakes State Park, 330-644-2220. Free for registered campers, $10 fee if not camping. Park is 7 miles west of I-77 Exit 133. From exit turn right on Lauby Rd; turn left of Greensburg Rd; go through Greensburg to E Nimisila Rd and turn left. Nimisila Rd will dead-end at Christman Rd. The campground is directly across Nimisila Rd at this intersection. The dump station is in the camping area on Nimisila Reservoir.

Bellevue	Lazy J Campground on US 20 about three miles west of town, $6
Celina	Mercer County Fairgrounds, 1001 W Market St, 419-586-3239, free. Dump station is in the northwest part of the fairgrounds near the horse barns. Latitude: 40.5497 · Longitude: -84.5834
Dalton	Citgo Bell Store at northeast corner of US 30 and OH 94, north side of parking lot, $5 or free with fuel purchase
Deersville	Tappan Lake Park, 1 1/2 miles north of town
Dover	Tuscarawas County Fairgrounds at 259 S Tuscarawas Ave
Galion	Craig Smith RV Center, 866-462-1746, Free
Lorain	Neff Brothers RV, 7475 Industrial Pkwy, 440-282-5600 or 888-647-1422, $5. From I-80/90 Exit 135, travel north on Baumhart Rd about three miles.
Mineral City	Atwood Lake Park, 9 miles southeast of town on Lakeview Rd (CR 114)
Sandusky	Accurate RV Sales & Service, 4305 Venice Rd, 419-624-8687, $6. Located one mile east of OH 2 and US 6 on the west side of Sandusky.
Streetsboro	All Seasons RV, 9043 SR-14, Streetsboro OH 44241 / 800-948-2100. Cost is $5. Dump station is located in back southwest corner of dealership. Open Mon-Sat, 9-5; closed Sun.
Sylvania	All American Coach Co., 419-885-4601, $8.50. Dealership is one mile east of US 23.
Tiffin	Dump station is just off OH 53 on the north side of town, no fee, site name is unknown
Toledo	Maumee Bay State Park, 419-836-7758, free if camping, $10 if not
Van Wert	Van Wert County Fairgrounds at 1055 S Washington St (US 127)
Zanesville	Wolfies Campground, 101 Buckeye Dr, Zanesville OH 43701 / 740-454-0925. Non-camper fee unknown

OKLAHOMA

Below is a list of RV dump stations in Oklahoma. Listed first are those easily accessed from Interstate highways followed by those in other locations throughout the state.

Interstate 35

Interstate 35 runs north to south for 236 miles from the Kansas state line to the Texas state line. Portions are also shared with I-40 and I-44. Northbound travelers should read up the chart. Southbound travelers read down the chart.

Exit(mm)	Description
185	US 77 / Perry
	Sooner's Corner Texaco
	▼ I-35 and I-44 run together / follows I-35 numbering ▼
137	NE 122nd St / Oklahoma City
	Flying J Travel Plaza
	Love's Travel Stop
	▲ I-35 and I-44 run together / follows I-35 numbering ▲
(59)	Rest Area

Interstate 40

Interstate 40 runs east to west for 331 miles from the Arkansas state line to the Texas state line. Part of it is shared with I-35. Eastbound travelers should read up the chart. Westbound travelers read down the chart.

Exit(mm)	Description
(316)	Rest Area (eb)
(314)	Welcome Center (wb)
264b	US 69 / to Eufaula
	Flying J Travel Plaza, 1255 W Gentry St, Checotah OK 74426 / 918-473-1243. Free. Latitude: 35.4750 • Longitude: -95.5386
(197)	Rest Area
142	Council Rd
	TA Travel Center

140	**Morgan Rd**
	Flying J Travel Plaza
	Pilot Travel Center
101	**US 281 / OK 8 / to Hinton**
	Hinton Travel Plaza
20	**US 283 / Sayre**
	Flying J Travel Plaza
(10)	Welcome Center (eb) / Rest Area (wb)
7	**OK 30 / Erick**
	Texaco Log Cabin
1	**Texola**
	Double D Fuel Stop

Interstate 44

Interstate 44 runs east to west for about 329 miles from the Missouri state line to the Texas state line. Part of it is shared with I-35. Much of I-44 is part of Oklahoma's toll-highway system. Eastbound travelers should read up the chart. Westbound travelers read down the chart.

Exit(mm)	Description
248	**OK 66 / OK 266**
	Dave's Claremore RV, 918-341-0114, Free. Dealer is three miles south of Claremore on Hwy 66. Dump station is in front of dealership and is well marked.
236a	**129th E Ave**
	Flying J Travel Plaza
▼ *I-35 and I-44 run together / follows I-35 numbering* ▼	
137	**NE 122nd St / Oklahoma City**
	Flying J Travel Plaza
	Love's Travel Stop
▲ *I-35 and I-44 run together / follows I-35 numbering* ▲	

Interstate 244

Interstate 244 is 15 miles long. It forms a partial loop around Tulsa. Exit numbering begins at West 51st Ave and increases in a clockwise direction.

Exit(mm)	Description
15	**129th E Ave**
	Flying J Travel Plaza

Other Locations

City or Town	Description
Ada	Twin Lakes RV, 14148 CR-1554, Ada OK 74820 / 580-399-9087 (call first). Commercial campground located southwest of town center along SR-1. Fee is the same as an overnight stay (currently $24). Latitude: 34.7611 · Longitude: -96.7033
Alva	Public dump station at the north end of city's swimming pool parking lot, near Hatfield Park at 14th St and W Flynn St, no charge. Latitude: 36.8063 · Longitude: -98.6804
Bartlesville	Phillips 66, 3315 SE Frank Phillips Blvd, 918-333-5540, Free. Latitude: 36.7507 · Longitude: -95.9384
Boise City	Love's Travel Stop at US 287 and US 56
Checotah	Flying J Travel Plaza at US 69 and US 266
Chouteau	Love's Travel Stop at US 412 and US 69
Colbert	Love's Travel Stop, 2150 Leavenworth Trail, Colbert OK 74730 / 580-296-5940. Free. Latitude: 33.9109 · Longitude: -96.4602
Colbert	Sherrard RV & KOA, 580-296-2485, $1
Cromwell	Four Winds Ranch, 405-944-1180, $5 for non-guests, free for overnight guests
Duncan	Doug's RV Center at US 81 and Fuller St, 580-252-7946, Free
Eufaula	Love's Travel Stop on US 69
Lawton	City of Lawton East-Side Park on Lake Lawtonka (city park) about ten miles west of I-44 Exit 45 via OK 49 and OK 58, free. Camping also available.
Miami	City park located along the Neosho River at 6th Ave SW and A St SW, one block west of S Main St (OK 125). Camping available, 14-day stay limit, drinking water, no electric hookups. Free.
Pauls Valley	Longmire City Lake about 14 miles east of town off OK 19
Pauls Valley	Pauls Valley City Lake about two miles northeast of town off OK 19
Woodward	Kevin's Corner Texaco at 3710 US 183

OREGON

Below is a list of RV dump stations in Oregon. Listed first are those easily accessed from Interstate highways followed by those in other locations throughout the state.

Interstate 5

Interstate 5 runs north to south for 308 miles from the Washington state line to the California state line. Northbound travelers should read up the chart. Southbound travelers read down the chart.

Exit(mm)	Description
199	**Coburg**
	TA Travel Center, $5 or free with fill-up.
136	**W Central Ave / Sutherlin**
	McGuffies BP Gas Station ($3 fee)
129	**OR 99 / Del Rio Rd**
	Kamper Korner RV Center, 541-673-1258, $3. From exit go north on Hwy 99 1 1/2 miles to dealership.
123	**Heritage Way / SW Portland Ave / Roseburg**
	Douglas County Fairgrounds ($3 fee)
119	**OR 99 / Roseburg**
	Love's Travel Stop
108	**Main St / Myrtle Creek**
	Millsite Park, 441 SW 4th Ave, Myrtle Creek OR 97457 / 541-863-3171. $5 fee. From exit, follow Main St to SW 4th Ave and turn right to park. Latitude: 43.0246 • Longitude: -123.2939
99	**Main St / Canyonville**
	Stanton County Park ($3 fee)
86	**Quines Creek Rd**
	Meadow Wood RV Park, 869 Autumn Ln, 800-606-1274, $5
	Comments: From southbound I-5 take Exit 86, go east over Interstate to dead end, right 3 miles to Barton Rd, left 500 feet to Autumn Ln, right one mile to park office.
83	**Barton Rd**
	Meadow Wood RV Park, 869 Autumn Ln, 800-606-1274, $5
	Comments: From northbound I-5 take Exit 83, right 500 feet to Autumn Ln, right one mile to park office.
58	**OR 99 / NE 6th St / Grants Pass**
	76 service station, 1995 NE 6th St, 541-474-9344, free

45b	**Valley of the Rogue State Park**
	Rest Area in Valley of the Rogue State Park
33	**E Pine St / Central Point**
	76 gas station on west side of highway, $2 or free with fill-up. Dump station is in the front.
27	**Barnett Rd / Medford**
	Shell Service Station, 428 E Barnett Rd, Medford OR 97501 / 541-779-2370. Cost is unknown
14	**OR 66 / Ashland St / Ashland**
	Shell service station, $5 fee or $3 with fuel purchase. Water available for washing tanks.

Interstate 84

I-84 runs east to west for approximately 378 miles from the Idaho state line to I-5 in Portland. Eastbound travelers should read up the chart. Westbound travelers read down the chart.

Exit(mm)	Description
376	**US 30 / Idaho Ave / Ontario**
	Pilot Travel Center
304	**OR 7 / Baker**
	Baker Truck Corral
	Jackson's Food Mart
(269)	Rest Area
209	**US 395 / OR 37 / Pendleton**
	Heritage Station Museum, 108 SW Frazer, no charge. Dump station is located in the southwest corner of the museum parking lot.
114	**LePage Park Rd / near Rufus**
	LePage Park (Corps of Engineers campground) at the mouth of the John Day River, 541-506-7816, $3; Golden Age Passport holders will receive a 50 percent discount.
(73)	Rest Area
63	**N 2nd St / Hood River**
	Hood River Waste Treatment Plant at 818 Riverside Dr

Interstate 205

Interstate 205 is a 37-mile route in Oregon and Washington. It forms an open loop around the Portland and Vancouver areas.

Exit(mm)	Description
9	**OR 99E / McLoughlin Ave / Oregon City**
	Clackamette RV Park (city park), 1955 Clackamette Dr, Oregon City OR 97045 / 505-657-0891. $5 fee.

Other Locations

City or Town	Description
Ashland	Howard Prairie Lake Resort, 3249 Hyatt Prairie Rd, 541-482-1979, $3. Resort is about 20 miles east of Ashland via Dead Indian Memorial Rd.
Astoria	Public dump station on Taylor Ave just north of the Youngs Bay Bridge. From the US 101 traffic circle (roundabout), exit east onto OR 202, then the very next left onto Taylor Ave. Taylor Ave is a short, one-way street parallel to US 101 going roughly north, which intersects back onto US 101. Easy access, even with a tow.
Bandon	Bullards Beach State Park on US 101 about two miles north of town
Bend	All Seasons RV & Marine, 63195 Jamison St, Bend OR 97708 / 800-285-5009. Cost is $5. Latitude: 44.0939 • Longitude: -121.3042
Bend	Expressway Market on Reed Market Rd east of US 97 at 15th St, $5 fee. Non-potable water available.
Bend	Texaco at 3rd St (US 97) and Revere Ave - $3 with fuel purchase
Brookings	Rest Area on US 101 about 2 miles north of Brookings at Harris Beach State Park
Burns	Rest Area on US 20 about 18 miles west of Burns
Canby	Professional Car Wash & Laundromat on S Birch St between Taco Bell and Burgerville, south side of OR 99E. $6 fee. Dump station is in back of laundromat by the car wash.
Chemult	A public dump station is located in the Walt Haring Snopark in Winema National Forest. Walt Haring Snopark is located one-half mile north of Chemult and one-half mile west of US 97 on Miller Lake Road (9772).
Coos Bay	Dump station is on US 101 in center of town ($1 honor pay)
Corvallis	Shell Food & Mart, 1680 SW 3rd St, 541-738-8028, Free. Located about one mile south of downtown area on Hwy 99W (SW 3rd St).
Elgin	Pacific Pride station, 2075 Public St, west side of town off OR 204, fee unknown.

Enterprise	Pacific Pride station, 317 Golf Course Rd, no charge. Located off OR 82, immediately to the north of the Safeway store on the west side of town.
Estacada	Public dump station near Timber Park off SR-224, north of town. Fee not known. Latitude: 45.2973 • Longitude: -122.3444
Eugene	Wastewater Treatment Plant on River Ave off the Beltline Road
Florence	Harbor Vista County Park about 3 miles north of town via US 101, 35th St, and N Rhododendron Dr, $3 fee
Florence	Jessie M. Honeyman State Park, on road to camping area before registration booth.
Florence	Port of Siuslaw RV Park & Marina, 100 Harbor St (east end of 1st St), 541-997-3040. Cost is $3. Latitude: 43.9684 • Longitude: -124.1019
Florence	Rest Area on US 101 about 14 miles north of Florence at C.G. Washburne State Park
Garibaldi	Barview Jetty Park on US 101 about 1 mile north of Garibaldi
Grand Ronde	Spirit Mountain Casino on SR-18 has a free dump station. Overnight dry camping is also free. Latitude: 45.0589 • Longitude: -123.5801
Hermiston	The Station at US 395 and W Catherine Ave, no fee, dump is near the porta potty
Hillsboro	Rock Creek Wastewater Treatment Plant, 3125 SE River Rd Hillsboro OR 97123 / 503-547-8000. Free. Open 24/7.
Hillsboro	Rock Creek Wastewater Treatment Plant at 3125 SE River Rd
Irrigon	Brown's Auto & Truck Stop on US 730 about 6 miles north of I-84 Exit 168
Island City	C&M Country Store at 10102 N Hwy 82
John Day	Rest Area on US 26 about 4 miles west of John Day at Clyde Holiday State Park
Joseph	Joseph Fire Station across from the rodeo grounds, free (donation requested)
Klamath Falls	Airport RV Storage, 2931 Bristal Ave, 541-273-0142, $5 or free to renters.
Klamath Falls	Klamath County Fairgrounds at 3531 S 6th St (OR 39) - $3 fee
Klamath Falls	Moore Park (city park) on Lakeshore Drive. Dump station is near the restrooms and boat dock. No charge. Water is available.
Klamath Falls	Suburban Self Storage at 3939 Hilyard Ave - from US 97 travel east of OR 39 to Summers Ln. Turn south and follow to Hilyard Ave - $3 fee

La Pine	Gordy's Truck Stop on east side of US 97 about three miles north of town, $6
La Pine	La Pine State Park, 15800 State Recreation Rd, 541-536-2071, 27 miles southwest of Bend and four miles west of US 97, no charge. GPS: 43.768452, -121.513399
Lebanon	Gills Landing Park (city park), 1400 E Grant St (across from River Park), $3. Park also has 21 RV sites with electricity for about $23 per night.
Madras	Public dump station adjacent to City Public Works; west on B St from US97/US 26 at north end of town. $3 donation requested
Madras	Tiger Mart Chevron & Mini Mart, 1210 SW Hwy 97, 541-475-7127, $4 or free with fuel purchase
McMinnville	Water Reclamation Facility at 3500 Clearwater Dr
Mill City	Riverbend Campground on OR 22, $3 fee
Molalla	Feyrer Park (county park), 3 miles southeast of Molalla on the Molalla River. Donation requested. Closed in winter. Latitude: 45.1384 • Longitude: -122.5349
Newberg	Public Works Department at OR 99W and W 3rd St, $1, fresh water available. Hours: Mon-Fri, 8am-4pm
Newport	Chamber of Commerce at US 101 and Fall St, east side of highway, free, non-potable water. Easy access from US 101. Turn east on Abby St (Apple Peddler Restaurant on east corner), make a left on 9th St and left on Fall St. Latitude: 44.6310 • Longitude: -124.0592
Newport	In parking lot south of Rogue Brewery, which is at the South Beach Marina underneath the south end of Yaquina Bay Bridge, no fee
Newport	South Beach State Park about 1 1/4 miles south of Yaquina Bridge on US 101, donations accepted.
Ontario	Malheur County Fairgrounds at 795 NW 9th St
Pacific City	Webb Park off Cape Kiwanda Dr about 1 mile north of Pacific City
Pendleton	In parking lot of train depot museum on Frazier Street between SE 2nd & SE 3rd, easy in and out, free, donations welcomed but not required
Philomath	Chevron Station on Main St (US 20) at S 14th St. The station has a sloping lot toward S 14th St, Turn south on S 14th St and swing wide making a full U-turn to the left. The dump is only a couple of feet east of the sidewalk, north of the propane tank. There is a short but steep pull to get back onto the highway or to the gas pump islands. Free. Latitude: 44.5398 • Longitude: -123.3661
Prineville	Crook County RV Park, 1040 S Main St, Prineville OR 97754 / 541-447-2599 or 800-609-2599. Cost is $4. Potable water is available. Latitude: 44.3034 • Longitude: -120.8406

Rainier	Wastewater treatment plant on US 30 next to city park, northwest end of town, no fee, difficult to use if towing a "toad"
Reedsport	Oregon Dunes NRA Visitor Center at north end of town at the junction of US 101 and OR 38, $3 fee.
Reedsport	Rest Area on US 101 about 8 miles south of Reedsport at William Tugman State Park
Roseburg	Gecko RV & Boat Storage, 350 Pomona St, Roseburg OR 97470 / 541-677-8400. Cost is $3. Located off OR 138 about 3 miles east of I-5 Exit 124. Gated entry; if an attendant is not available, call the posted number for entry.
Scappoose	Jackpot/Exxon Station on US-30, $3 fee
Shady Cove	Chevron Station, 21222 Hwy 62, no charge, non-potable water available for rinsing. Latitude: 42.6081 • Longitude: -122.8147
Sisters	Three Sisters Overnight Park (city park) on the southeast side of town off US 20. 60-site campground ($10), $5 for dump station use. Latitude: 44.2883 • Longitude: -121.5425
Sweet Home	Sweet Home RV Center, 4691 US 20, 541-367-4293, $5
Tigard	Durham Wastewater Treatment Plant at 16580 SW 85th Ave, free. From I-5 Exit 290, go west one block to SW 72nd Ave and turn right; north one block to SW Durham Rd and turn left; follow about one mile to SW 85th Ave and turn left.
Tillamook	Trask Park on Trask River Rd about 14 miles east of Tillamook
Toledo	A public dump station is located at the Georgia Pacific Paper Mill off US 20 in Toledo. It is by Gate 3 and contractor parking lot. A fee of .25 is charged for water.
Ukiah	Public dump station located behind central park on State St, one block south of Main St, Free. Dump area has fresh water; use your own hose for drinking water.
Unity	Rest Area on OR 245 at Unity Lake State Park
Vernonia	Anderson Park (city park), 450 Jefferson Ave, 503-429-2531, $5. 19 RV sites with full hookups also available.
Parkdale	Toll Bridge County Park on OR 35 east of Parkdale
Winchester Bay	Salmon Harbor County Park on Ork Rock Rd between boat basins. From US 101, turn right onto 9th St, then onto Ork Rock Rd. Cost is $3.
Woodburn	Waste Treatment Plant at 2815 Molalla Rd (OR 211)

PENNSYLVANIA

Below is a list of RV dump stations in Pennsylvania. Listed first are those easily accessed from Interstate highways followed by those in other locations throughout the state.

Interstate 70

I-70 runs east to west for about 173 miles from the Maryland state line to the West Virginia state line. Portions are also shared with I-76, I-79, and the Pennsylvania Turnpike. Eastbound travelers should read up the chart. Westbound travelers read down the chart.

Exit(mm)	Description
49	**Smithton**
	Flying J Travel Plaza, 122 Fitz Henry Rd, Smithton PA 15479 / 724-872-4050. Free. Latitude: 40.1700 • Longitude: -79.7327

Interstate 76

Interstate 76 runs east to west for about 350 miles from the New Jersey state line to the Ohio state line. Nearly all of I-76 is also the Pennsylvania Turnpike. Part of the Interstate is also shared with I-70. Eastbound travelers should read up the chart. Westbound travelers read down the chart.

Exit(mm)	Description
(325)	Rest Area (eb)
(259)	Rest Area (wb)

Interstate 78

Interstate 78 in Pennsylvania runs east to west for about 77 miles from the New Jersey state line to Interstate 81 Exit 89 near Jonestown.

Exit(mm)	Description
26b	**PA 61 N / Hamburg**
	Cabela's, 100 Cabela Dr, Hamburg PA 19526 / 610-929-7000. Free. Located north of exit. Latitude: 40.5580 • Longitude: -76.0031

Comments: Cabela's has a huge parking lot with lots of RV parking. Overnight RV parking is not allowed.

Interstate 80

Interstate 80 runs east to west for 311 miles from the New Jersey state line to the Ohio state line. Eastbound travelers should read up the chart. Westbound travelers read down the chart.

Exit(mm)	Description
173	**PA 64 / Lamar / to Mill Hall**
	Flying J Travel Plaza, 570-726-4080
78	**PA 36 / Brookville**
	Flying J Travel Plaza
	TA Travel Center

Interstate 81

Interstate 81 runs north to south 233 miles from the New York state line to the Maryland state line. Northbound travelers should read up the chart. Southbound travelers read down the chart.

Exit(mm)	Description
219	**PA 848 / to Gibson**
	Flying J Travel Plaza
178b	**Avoca / to US 11**
	Petro Stopping Center
52	**US 11 / Carlisle**
	Flying J Travel Plaza, 1501 Harrisburg Pike, Carlisle PA 17013 / 717-243-6659. Cost is $10 or $5 with Flying J card. No rinse water. Latitude: 40.2342 • Longitude: -77.1226

Interstate 90

Interstate 90 runs east to west for 46 miles from the New York state line to the Ohio state line. Eastbound travelers should read up the chart. Westbound travelers read down the chart.

Exit(mm)	Description
35	**PA 531 / to Harborcreek**
	TA Travel Center

Interstate 276

Interstate 276 near Philadelphia is about 33 miles long. It runs east to west from the New Jersey state line to I-76. It is also part of the Pennsylvania Turnpike. Eastbound travelers should read up the chart. Westbound travelers read down the chart.

Exit(mm)	Description
(351)	Welcome Center (wb) / Rest Area (eb)

Other Locations

City or Town	Description
Austin	Austin Campground, 364 Nelson Run Rd, Austin PA 16720 / 814-647-8777 or 800-878-0889. Free if camping, $10 if not. Latitude: 41.5667 • Longitude: -78.0233
Breezewood	TA Travel Center off the Pennsylvania Turnpike at Exit 161. Phone number is 814-735-2011. Cost is unknown. See the TA Fuel Desk Attendant for instructions.
Coudersport	Potter County Family Campground, 3075 E 2nd St (US 6), 814-274-5010, $8. Campground is 8 miles east of town on US Hwy 6.
Dallas	Bryant's RV Showcase on PA 415, $5 fee, drop box for fee after hours
Ephrata	222 Travel Plaza at US 222 and US 322
Milroy	Unimart on US 322
Uniontown	Wastewater treatment plant at 90 Romeo Ln near junction of US 119 and PA 51, no fee
Willow Street	Mellott Brothers RV, 2718 Willow Street Pike, 800-826-3556 or 717-464-2311, $2

Rhode Island

Below is a list of RV dump stations in Rhode Island. Listed first are those easily accessed from Interstate highways followed by those in other locations throughout the state.

Interstate 95

Interstate 95 runs north to south for 43 miles from the Massachusetts state line to the Connecticut state line. Exit numbers are based on the consecutive numbering system. Northbound travelers should read up the chart. Southbound travelers read down the chart.

Exit(mm)	Description
8	**RI 2 / Quaker Ln / East Greenwich** Arlington RV, 966 Quaker Ln, 401-884-7550, open Mon thru Sat 8am to 5pm, $5 fee. Northbound travelers use Exit 8b. Latitude: 41.6709 • Longitude: -71.4993

Other Locations

City or Town	Description
Woonsocket	Woonsocket Wastewater Treatment Plant behind the Fire Station on Cumberland Hill Rd. No charge. Dump cover is usually locked; you'll need to find an employee to unlock the cap. Latitude: 42.0024 • Longitude: -71.4968

SOUTH CAROLINA

Below is a list of RV dump stations in South Carolina. Listed first are those easily accessed from Interstate highways followed by those in other locations throughout the state.

Interstate 20

Interstate 20 runs east to west for 142 miles from I-95 near Florence to the Georgia state line. Eastbound travelers should read up the chart. Westbound travelers read down the chart.

Exit(mm)	Description
70	**US 321 / Fairfield Rd**
	Flying J Travel Plaza

Interstate 26

Interstate 26 in South Carolina is an east-west route that is 221 miles long. It runs from US 17 in Charleston to the North Carolina state line. Eastbound travelers should read up the chart. Westbound travelers read down the chart.

Exit(mm)	Description
205a	**US 78 / University Blvd**
	KOA campground one mile west of exit on US 78, $10
16	**John Dodd Rd / Spartanburg**
	Camping World, 114 Best Dr, Spartanburg SC 29303 / 866-999-3164. Cost is $5; free if club member. Latitude: 35.0108 • Longitude: -82.0268

Interstate 77

Interstate 77 runs north to south for 91 miles from the North Carolina state line to I-26 in Columbia. Northbound travelers should read up the chart. Southbound travelers read down the chart.

Exit(mm)	Description
83	**Sutton Rd / Fort Mill**
	Love's Travel Stop, Fort Mill SC 29708 / 803-802-7130. Free. Latitude: 34.9982 • Longitude: -80.9761
73	**SC 901 / Mt Holly Rd / to Rock Hill**
	Flying J, 2435 Mt Holly Rd, 803-328-5700, Free
34	**SC 34 / Ridgeway**
	Ridgeway Campground, 7210 Hwy 34 E, Ridgeway SC 29130 / 803-337-8585. $7. Campground is east of exit.

Interstate 85

Interstate 85 runs north to south for 106 miles from the North Carolina state line to the Georgia state line. Northbound travelers should read up the chart. Southbound travelers read down the chart.

Exit(mm)	Description
90	**SC 105 / Hyatt St / Gaffney**
	Pilot Travel Center, 909 Hyatt St, 864-206-0050, Free. Latitude: 35.0787 • Longitude: -81.7029

Interstate 95

Interstate 95 runs north to south for 198 miles from the North Carolina state line to the Georgia state line. Northbound travelers should read up the chart. Southbound travelers read down the chart.

Exit(mm)	Description
181	**SC 38 / Oak Grove**
	Flying J Travel Plaza
	Wilco Travel Plaza
169	**TV Rd / to Florence**
	Petro Stopping Center

119	**SC 261 / Manning**
	TA Travel Center

Other Locations

City or Town	Description
Goose Creek	Lower Berkeley Wastewater Treatment Plant at 2111 Red Bank Rd
Greenville	Paris Mountain State Park, $6. The park is reached through a residential area but is clearly marked. Pay when entering the park. Mark on the envelope "dumping only."
Lexington	Edmund RV Park, 5920 Edmund Hwy, 803-955-4010, $5 fee. From I-20 Exit 55 follow SC 6 south for 7 miles. From I-26 Exit 113 follow SC 302 south for about 9 miles.
Ninety Six	Lake Greenwood State Recreation Area, 302 State Park Rd, Ninety Six SC 29666 / 864-543-3535. Free. Latitude: 34.1733 • Longitude: -82.0216
Seneca	High Falls County Park about 13 miles north of town via SC 130 and SC 183
Seneca	South Cove County Park about 4 miles north of Seneca via SC 28 and SC 188
Westminster	Chau Ram County Park 3 miles west of town on US 76

SOUTH DAKOTA

Below is a list of RV dump stations in South Dakota. Listed first are those easily accessed from Interstate highways followed by those in other locations throughout the state.

Interstate 29

Interstate 29 runs north to south for 253 miles from the North Dakota state line to the Iowa state line. Northbound travelers should read up the chart. Southbound travelers read down the chart.

Exit(mm)	Description
213	**SD 15 / to Wilmot**
	Rest Area east of exit
177	**US 212 / Watertown**
	Stone's Truck Stop
(161)	Rest Area
121	**CR B / 223rd St**
	Rest Area east of exit
83	**SD 38 / W 60th St / Sioux Falls**
	Flying J Travel Plaza
26	**SD 50 / Vermillion**
	Welcome Center east of exit

Interstate 90

Interstate 90 runs east to west for 413 miles from the Minnesota state line to the Wyoming state line. Eastbound travelers should read up the chart. Westbound travelers read down the chart.

Exit(mm)	Description
(412)	Welcome Center (wb)
(363)	Rest Area
332	**SD 37 / Mitchell**
	Cabela's, 601 Cabella Dr, Mitchell SD 57301 / 605-996-0337. Free.
	Latitude: 43.6906 • Longitude: -98.0172
(302)	Rest Area (wb)
(301)	Rest Area (eb)
(264)	Rest Area

(221)	Rest Area (wb)
(218)	Rest Area (eb)
(167)	Rest Area (wb)
(165)	Rest Area (eb)
(100)	Rest Area
98	**Baseline Rd / Wasta**
	BP 24 Express, $5
66	**Box Elder**
	Flying J Travel Plaza
61	**Elk Vale Rd**
	Flying J Travel Plaza
58	**N Haines Ave**
	Conoco
55	**Deadwood Ave**
	Windmill Truck Stop
(42)	Rest Area
30	**SD 34 / US 14A / Sturgis**
	Cenex Station
(1)	Welcome Center (eb)

Other Locations

City or Town	Description
Armour	Lion's Park on east side of US 281 in town, donations accepted
Belle Fourche	Chamber of Commerce at 415 5th Ave (US 85)
Brookings	Sexauer Park at Western Ave and 8th St. This city park also has 13 campsites with electric hookups.
Buffalo	City park just south of town on west side of US 85. Dump, rinse, and fresh water available, free. Park also has restrooms, picnic shelter, and free overnight camping.
Burke	Public dump station behind Pump & Stuff convenience store on US 18 in town, no fee.
Custer	Broken Arrow Campground, 25458 Flynn Creek Rd, 605-673-4471, fee not known. Latitude: 43.7147 • Longitude: -103.5788
Deadwood	Ken's Camper Sales on Hwy 14A between Deadwood and Lead
Flandreau	Flandreau City Park one mile east of town, camping for less than $10 per day. Watch your height when entering the gate. There is a bypass available to avoid the gate.

Huron	Memorial Park (city park) campground, 10 Jersey Ave, free if camping, $3 if not camping. From US 14, turn south on Jersey Ave at the "world's largest pheasant." Campground has nice paved walking trails, golf, pool, etc. Latitude: 44.3655 • Longitude: -98.1980
Ipswich	Collier's Park at US 12 and 9th St, no charge
Madison	Free dump and potable water at Flynn Field Park at SW 8th St and S Egan Ave. From the corner of Washington and SD-34 (Prostrollo AutoMall), go one block west on SD-34. Go right (N) on S Egan Ave and take the first left (W) on SW 8th St. Dump station will be on the right. Nicely maintained facility. Latitude: 43.9966 • Longitude: -97.1163
Pierre	Griffin City Park on Missouri Ave along riverfront about 3 blocks south of Dakota Ave. Free. 15 RV sites with hookups also available.
Webster	City park 1/2 block east of SH-25, south side of US-12. Free/donation requested.
Wolsey	281 Travel Center on US 14/281 at mile marker 331

TENNESSEE

Below is a list of RV dump stations in Tennessee. Listed first are those easily accessed from Interstate highways followed by those in other locations throughout the state.

Interstate 40

I-40 runs east to west for about 455 miles from the North Carolina state line to the Arkansas state line. Portions are also shared with I-24 and I-75. Eastbound travelers should read up the chart. Westbound travelers read down the chart.

Exit(mm)	Description
▼ I-40 and I-75 run together / follows I-40 numbering ▼	
369	**Watt Rd / near Farragut**
	Flying J Travel Plaza, 800 Watt Rd, 865-531-7400, free. Enter at first entry (not truck entrance); dump station is immediately to the left. Once dumped you can move forward to fill LP tank. Latitude: 35.8816 • Longitude: -84.2358
	Petro Stopping Center, 865-693-6542. Dump station is at left front side of parking lot. Free
▲ I-40 and I-75 run together / follows I-40 numbering ▲	
288	**TN 111 / Cookeville**
	Middle Tennessee Auto & Truck Plaza
182	**TN 96 / to Dickson**
	Flying J Travel Plaza
172	**TN 46 / to Dickson**
	Pilot Travel Center
87	**US 70 / US 412 / Jackson**
	Love's Travel Stop

Interstate 75

Interstate 75 in Tennessee runs north to south for 162 miles from the Kentucky state line to the Georgia state line. Portions are shared with I-640 and I-40. Northbound travelers should read up the chart. Southbound travelers read down the chart.

Exit(mm)	Description
	▼ *I-40 and I-75 run together / follows I-40 numbering* ▼
369	**Watt Rd / near Farragut** Flying J Travel Plaza, 800 Watt Rd, 865-531-7400, free. Enter at first entry (not truck entrance); dump station is immediately to the left. Once dumped you can move forward to fill LP tank. Latitude: 35.8816 • Longitude: -84.2358 Petro Stopping Center, 865-693-6542. Dump station is at left front side of parking lot. Free
	▲ *I-40 and I-75 run together / follows I-40 numbering* ▲
49	**TN 30 / Decatur Pike / Athens** Athens I-75 Campground, 2509 Decatur Pike, 423-745-9199, $6

Interstate 81

Interstate 81 runs north to south for 76 miles from the Virginia state line to I-40 near Dandridge. Northbound travelers should read up the chart. Southbound travelers read down the chart.

Exit(mm)	Description
63	**TN 357 / Airport Pkwy / near Blountville** Bristol/Kingsport KOA, 425 Rocky Branch Rd, 423-323-7790, $20. Open during business hours only. Latitude: 36.5110 • Longitude: -82.4396
4	**TN 341 / White Pine** Pilot Travel Center

Other Locations

City or Town	Description
Chattanooga	Chester Frost Park (county park) off Hixson Pike (TN 319) about 5 miles north of TN 153. There are four dump stations, three are off the main drive before you approach the camping areas. These are "in a line" so if someone is using one, you may have to wait to get to an unused station. The fourth is more distant, sheltered, and easily accessible. No fee is charged.
Kingsport	Wastewater Treatment Plant at 620 W Industry Dr (free)
Knoxville	Southlake RV Park, 3730 Maryville Pike (TN 33), 865-573-1837, $5 fee, Good Sam Park
Morristown	Cherokee Park (county park), 3075 Floyd Hall Rd, 423-586-5232, Free if camping, $4 if not. Park is about five miles north of downtown via US 25E. From US 25E turn east at traffic light onto Cherokee Park Rd; left on Floyd Hall Rd to park.
Tazewell	Exxon station at 1446 N Broad St
Tellico Plains	KOA, 7310 Hwy 360, 423-253-2447, $10

TEXAS

Below is a list of RV dump stations in Texas. Listed first are those easily accessed from Interstate highways followed by those in other locations throughout the state.

Interstate 10

Interstate 10 runs east to west for 881 miles from the Louisiana state line to the New Mexico state line. Part of it is shared with I-35. Eastbound travelers should read up the chart. Westbound travelers read down the chart.

Exit(mm)	Description
873	**TX 62 / TX 73 / to Bridge City**
	Flying J Travel Plaza
789	**Thompson Rd / Baytown**
	Flying J Travel Plaza, 1876 E Freeway, Baytown TX 77521 / 281-424-7226. Free. Latitude: 29.7960 • Longitude: -95.0347
	TA Travel Center, Baytown TX 77521 / 281-424-7772. Free. Latitude: 29.7960 • Longitude: -95.0310
737	**Pederson Rd / Katy**
	Love's Travel Stop, 612 Pederson Rd, 281-391-5556, free. Latitude: 29.7794 • Longitude: -95.8813
(590)	Rest Area
583	**Foster Rd**
	Flying J Travel Plaza
	TA Travel Center
(514)	Rest Area
(394)	Rest Area
372	**Taylor Box Rd**
	Circle Bar Auto & Truck Plaza
212	**TX 17 / FM 2448 / to Pecos**
	I-10 Fina
138	**Broadway / Van Horn**
	Eagles Nest RV Park, 1605 W Broadway, Van Horn TX 79855 / 432-283-2420. Cost is $10.
0	**FM 1905 / Anthony**
	Flying J Travel Plaza, 3001 Mountain Pass Blvd, 915-886-2737. Latitude: 31.9966 • Longitude: -106.5802
	Pilot Travel Center

Interstate 20

Interstate 20 runs east to west for 636 miles from the Louisiana state line to I-10 near Kent. Eastbound travelers should read up the chart. Westbound travelers read down the chart.

Exit(mm)	Description
540	**S Oak St / Van**
	Love's Travel Stop, 1221 S Oak St, 903-963-7341, Free. Dump station at truck entrance on north side of store. Easy entrance and exit. Latitude: 32.5088 • Longitude: -95.6428
503	**Wilson Rd**
	Rip Griffin Travel Center
472	**Bonnie View Rd**
	Flying J Travel Plaza
	TA Travel Center
466	**S Polk St**
	Love's Travel Stop
277	**FM 707 / Tye**
	Flying J Travel Plaza
42	**US 285 / Pecos**
	Flying J Travel Plaza

Interstate 27

I-27 runs north to south for 124 miles from Amarillo to Lubbock. Northbound travelers should read up the chart. Southbound travelers read down the chart.

Exit(mm)	Description
14	**FM 1729**
	New Deal Truck Stop
4	**4th St / US 82 / Lubbock**
	Flying J Travel Plaza, 602 4th St, 806-744-0539, Free. Latitude: 33.5930 • Longitude: -101.8410

Interstate 30

Interstate 30 runs east to west for 224 miles from the Arkansas state line to I-20, west of Fort Worth. Eastbound travelers should read up the chart. Westbound travelers read down the chart.

Exit(mm)	Description
70	**FM 549**
	Love's Travel Stop
68	**TX 205 / Rockwall**
	TA Travel Center, 972-722-7450, fee unknown

Interstate 35

Interstate 35 runs north to south for 504 miles from the Oklahoma state line to Laredo. I-35 splits into I-35E and I-35W near Hillsboro and comes together again in Denton. Northbound travelers should read up the chart. Southbound travelers read down the chart.

Exit(mm)	Description
496b	**W California St / Gainesville**
	City park east of exit, donations accepted. Park also has campsites with full hookups.
	Rumpy's Valero Truck Stop, 801 N I-35, 940-612-1121, Free. Truck stop is on the west frontage road between I-35 Exits 496 and 498. Dump station is at rear of property. Very clean and accessible for big rigs.
444	**Sandy Lake Rd / Whitlock Ln / Carrollton**
	Sandy Lake RV & Mobile Home Park, 1915 Sandy Lake Rd, 972-242-6808, fee not known.
368a	**TX 22 / TX 171 / to Whitney**
	Love's Travel Stop
331	**New Rd**
	Flying J Travel Plaza
328	**FM 2063 / FM 2113 / Moody**
	Pilot Travel Center
193	**Conrads Rd / Kohlenberg Rd**
	Rip Griffin Travel Center
(180)	Rest Area

144	Fischer Rd
	Love's Travel Stop
(130)	Rest Area

Interstate 35W

Interstate 35W runs north to south for 85 miles. It splits from I-35 near Hillsboro and rejoins I-35 in Denton. Northbound travelers should read up the chart. Southbound travelers read down the chart.

Exit(mm)	Description
40	Garden Acres Dr
	Love's Travel Stop

Interstate 37

Interstate 37 in Texas runs north to south for 143 miles from San Antonio to Corpus Christi. Northbound travelers should read up the chart. Southbound travelers read down the chart.

Exit(mm)	Description
130	Southton Rd / Elmendorf
	Braunig Lake RV Resort, 13550 Dunop Rd, Elmendorf TX 78112 / 877-633-3170. Cost is $5. Latitude: 29.2855 • Longitude: -98.3939

Interstate 40

Interstate 40 runs east to west for 177 miles from the Oklahoma state line to the New Mexico state line. Eastbound travelers should read up the chart. Westbound travelers read down the chart.

Exit(mm)	Description
76	TX 468 Spur / to Airport
	Flying J Travel Plaza
75	TX 335 Loop / Lakeside Rd
	Pilot Travel Center
74	Whitaker Rd
	Love's Travel Stop
	TA Travel Center
36	US 385 / Vega
	Texas Quick Stop

Interstate 45

Interstate 45 runs north to south for about 286 miles from Dallas to TX Highway 87 in Galveston. Northbound travelers should read up the chart. Southbound travelers read down the chart.

Exit(mm)	Description
272	**Fulghum Rd / near Hutchins**
	Love's Travel Stop, 972-225-3560, free. Latitude: 32.6221 • Longitude: -96.6931
	Comments: Pull into the automobile area instead of the truck area. Located at south end of lot.
238	**FM 1603**
	Corner Food Mart
198	**FM 27 / to Wortham**
	Love's Travel Stop
64	**Richey Rd**
	Flying J Travel Plaza
1c	**Teichman Rd / Galveston**
	Harborside Food Mart

Other Locations

City or Town	Description
Borger	Huber Park (city) located at south end of Main St at Pine St, free, easy access and ample turn-around space. RV parking spaces also available, sites are back in and paved with water and electric hookups.
Breckenridge	City park on E Walker St (US 180)
Brownfield	Coleman Park (city park) off US 62, donation requested. From US 62 go east one block on Reppto St E and then south one block on First St S. Park has 12 campsites with water and electric hookups; 4-day limit.
Buffalo	Holland Ranch RV Park, 2144 FM 1618, 903-322-1204, $5. From town, follow TX 75 south about 8 miles to FM 1618 and then east one mile. Latitude: 31.3650 • Longitude: -95.9864
Corpus Christi	Padre Island National Seashore. Follow S Padre Island Dr from town. The dump station and water fill are at the entrance of the campground, which is near the visitor center. Must pay entrance fee of $10 before entering.

Decatur	Allsup's at 1305 US 287
Del Rio	Diablo East Marina, approximately 8 miles west of Del Rio off US 90. Site provided free of charge by the National Park Service.
Dumas	Texhoma Park (city park) on US 87 west end of town. The city provides free overnight camping spaces with electricity at each site. There is also a free (donation accepted) dump station and water at the south end of park.
Edinburg	Love's Travel Stop northbound US 281 at exit for FM 2812, 956-316-1782
Edna	Love's Travel Stop at US 59 and Milby Road
Floydada	Wayne Russell RV Park (city park) on US 70, north side of town, 806-983-2834, no charge. Latitude: 33.9933 • Longitude: -101.3418
Frisco	Hidden Cove Park, 20400 Hackberry Creek Park Rd, 972-294-1443, free if camping, $15 with Hidden Cove's Annual car pass or $25 without the pass.
Giddings	South Forty RV Park, 3689 S Hwy 77, 979-366-9341, $5. Easy in and out for big rigs. Dump station located across from the club house/pool. Large rigs find it easier to pull on through the park as the dump is designed for use on exit. Latitude: 30.0956 • Longitude: -96.9121
Gilmer	RV park at the Yamboree grounds on US 271 north of town
Graham	Fireman's City Park on TX 67. Also has 28 RV sites with hookups.
Graham	Lake Eddelman City Park on US 380. Also has 12 RV sites with hookups.
Hawkins	Lake Hawkins RV Park (county park), 903-769-4545, $2. Go west 3 miles on US 80 and one mile north on Hwy 3440.
Iowa Park	Rest Areas on US 287 (Northwest Freeway), both directions of travel, no fee, northwest of Wichita Falls. Latitude: 33.9657 • Longitude: -98.7133
Jacksonville	Lake Jacksonville Recreation Area about 3 miles southwest of town
Kingsville	Love's Travel Stop, 361-592-7210, located at the corner of Corral St and US 77, free
Lamesa	City park about four blocks south of US 180 on the west side of town, free. Also has eight campsites with hookups for RVers.
Lampasas	Public dump station in city park on US 281, no fee

Littlefield	Waylon Jennings Free RV Park on US 385, 806-385-5161 (city hall), Free. Park also has a campground with over 100 campsites.
Lubbock	Chisum Travel Center, one mile outside Loop 289 on US 84, free
Lubbock	Diamond Shamrock convenience store, 5720 Spur 327, 806-799-5303, Free. Store is located in southwest edge of city on the northeast corner of Spur 327 and Frankford Ave.
Lufkin	Love's Travel Stop at TX 287 and Ford Chapel Rd (FM 841)
Mason	Mason city park one mile south of town square. Turn into city park/golf course from US 87; at first intersection amid golf course, take 45 degree angle left turn into second group of RV sites; dump is on left. Can handle all size rigs. Several budget RV sites available in park with water, electric and sewer.
Mineola	Civic Center at 1150 N Newsom St one block east of US 69
Odem	Odem Truck Stop at 1206 US 77
Perryton	Wigham city park on Main St (US 83) between SE 9th Ave and SE 11th Ave, RV sites with hookups available
Quitman	Jim Hogg City Park just south of Wood County Courthouse on TX 37
Rosenberg	Cottonwood Travel Plaza, 2801 US Hwy 59, 281-238-0066, free. Potable water available.
Shepherd	Champion Travel Plaza at US 59 and FM 2914
Stephenville	City park just off the downtown square on Graham St (TX 108), 1/2 mile north of US 67/US 377 S Loop
Sweetwater	Nolan County Coliseum, 1699 Cypress St, Sweetwater TX 79556 / 326-235-3484. Latitude 32.4842 • Longitude: -100.4129
Texas City	Wastewater treatment plant near the Texas City Dike, free.
Turkey	Public dump station 1/2 block north of main drag at the rear of a John Deere implement dealership. Fresh water is available. No charge.
Waller	Love's Travel Stop at US 290 and FM 2920
Wichita Falls	Wichita River Bend RV Park (city park), 300 Central Freeway, 940-761-7490. Adjacent to the travel information center. Accessible from I-44 at exit 1C. Has 28 campsites with hookups for $10 per night. Not known if there is a fee for dump station use if not camping.
Winnsboro	City park on Hope Ln near junction of FM 515 (E Coke Rd) and FM 852 (Gilmer Rd).

UTAH

Below is a list of RV dump stations in Utah. Listed first are those easily accessed from Interstate highways followed by those in other locations throughout the state.

Interstate 15

Interstate 15 runs north to south for about 403 miles from the Idaho state line to the Arizona state line. Parts are shared with I-80 and I-84. Northbound travelers should read up the chart. Southbound travelers read down the chart.

Exit(mm)	Description
▼ I-15 and I-84 run together / follows I-15 numbering ▼	
362	**US 91 / Brigham City**
	Flying J Travel Plaza
357	**UT 315 / to Willard**
	Flying J Travel Plaza
343	**UT 104 / 21st St / Ogden**
	Flying J Travel Plaza
▲ I-15 and I-84 run together / follows I-15 numbering ▲	
328	**W 200 N / Kaysville**
	Blaine Jensen & Sons RV Center, 780 N 900 W, 800-281-2799, no charge
316	**UT 68 / Bountiful / Woods Cross**
	RB's One Stop
▼ I-15 and I-80 run together / follows I-15 numbering ▼	
305b	**UT 201 / 21st St / 13th St / Salt Lake City**
	Flying J Travel Plaza
▲ I-15 and I-80 run together / follows I-15 numbering ▲	
284	**UT-92 / Lehi**
	Cabela's, 2502 W Grand Terrace Pkwy, Lehi UT 84043 / 801-766-2500. Free. Latitude: 40.4371 • Longitude: -111.8894
250	**UT 115 / Payson**
	Flying J Travel Plaza, 840 N Main, 801-465-9281, free
222	**UT 28 / Nephi**
	Circle C Car & Truck Plaza
	Flying J Travel Plaza
	Tri-Mart Fuel Stop

78	**UT 141 / Parowan**
	TA Travel Center
8	**Saint George Blvd**
	Premium Oil

Interstate 70

Interstate 70 runs east to west for 232 miles from the Colorado state line to I-15 exit 132 near Beaver. Eastbound travelers should read up the chart. Westbound travelers read down the chart.

Exit(mm)	Description
164	**UT 19 / Green River**
	West Winds Truck Stop
160	**UT 19 / Green River**
	West Winds Truck Stop
40	**Main St / Richfield**
	Flying J Travel Plaza

Interstate 80

Interstate 80 runs east to west for 197 miles from the Wyoming state line to the Nevada state line. Part of it is also I-15. Eastbound travelers should read up the chart. Westbound travelers read down the chart.

Exit(mm)	Description
162	**Coalville**
	Holiday Hills RV Park, Coalville UT 84017 / 435-336-4421. Cost is $3.
	▼ *I-15 and I-80 run together / follows I-15 numbering* ▼
305b	**UT 201 / 21st St / 13th St / Salt Lake City**
	Flying J Travel Plaza
	▲ *I-15 and I-80 run together / follows I-15 numbering* ▲
99	**UT 36 / to Tooele**
	Flying J Travel Plaza
	TA Travel Center

Interstate 84

Interstate 84 runs east to west for about 120 miles from I-80 near Coalville to the Idaho state line. Portions are shared with I-15. Eastbound travelers should read up the chart. Westbound travelers read down the chart.

Exit(mm)	Description
103	**State St / Morgan**
	7-Eleven, 404 E 300 N, Morgan UT / 801-829-3639. Free. Latitude: 41.0449 • Longitude: -111.6762
	▼ *I-15 and I-84 run together / follows I-15 numbering* ▼
343	**UT 104 / 21st St / Ogden**
	Flying J Travel Plaza
357	**UT 315 / to Willard**
	Flying J Travel Plaza
362	**US 91 / Brigham City**
	Flying J Travel Plaza
	▲ *I-15 and I-84 run together / follows I-15 numbering* ▲
40	**UT 102 / Tremonton / Bothwell**
	Golden Spike Travel Plaza
7	**Snowville**
	Flying J Travel Plaza

Interstate 215

Interstate 215 is 29 miles long. It forms a partial loop around Salt Lake City. Exit numbers increase in a clockwise direction.

Exit(mm)	Description
18	**UT 171 / West Valley City**
	State Trailer Supply, 3600 S Redwood Rd, 801-978-0400. From exit go east on UT 171 to Redwood Rd and turn south. This is a very large RV supply store with several large repair and installation bays. Free
28	**UT 68 / Redwood Rd**
	Flying J Travel Plaza

Other Locations

City or Town	Description
Clinton	Public dump station just northeast of Wal-Mart at 1632 N 2000 W, fee unknown
Duchesne	Gateway 66, 655 W Main St (US 40)
Escalante	Escalante Petrified Forest State Park, 710 North Reservoir Rd, Escalante UT 84726 / 435-826-4466. Fee not known.
Hurricane	Little Creek Station, 4105 S Hwy 59, 435-877-1101, fee unknown. The dump is located at the rear of the parking lot.
Jensen	Dinosaur Gifts & Souvenirs, $3. Located at the store just outside Dinosaur National Monument (Quarry entrance). Fee waived with store purchase. Closed in winter.
Kanab	Samco on US 89/89A at 289 S 100 E
Logan	Logan fairgrounds, west of US 89 near intersection of W 500 S and S 500 W, $5. On west side of fairgrounds, just north of Armory.
Moab	Quality RV Service & Supply, 850 S US 191, $5 fee, on west side of street 1/2 block south of McDonald's, 24-hour access, pay on honor system after business hours, potable water available (shut off after business hours in winter), pull-thru access for vehicles as large as 75 feet long
Price	Public dump station at fairgrounds. Take Exit 240 on US 6 at UT 55 / W 100 N and follow signs uphill to fairgrounds.
Price	Sinclair Gas Station, 850 Carbon Ave, Price UT 84501. Free. Latitude: 39.5863 • Longitude: -110.8130
Saint George	Premium Oil at 181 UT 18 just north of UT 34
Sandy	Cottonwood Improvement District, 8620 Highland Dr, Sandy UT 84093 / 801-943-7671. Free. The dump is located in the sewer company's parking lot at the corner of Alta Canyon Rd and Highland Dr. Alta Canyon Rd is about 3 miles south of I-215 Exit 8. Latitude: 40.5940 • Longitude: -111.8325
Tooele	Public dump station on SR-36 at the south end of town; located adjacent to the State Fuel Depot at 9th S and SR-36. Fee unknown. Latitude: 40.5142 • Longitude: -112.3101
West Valley	Granger Hunter Improvement District, 3000 S 3600 W, West Valley City UT 84119 / 801-968-3551. Free. Latitude: 40.7068 • Longitude: -111.9773

VERMONT

Below is a list of RV dump stations in Vermont. Listed first are those easily accessed from Interstate highways followed by those in other locations throughout the state.

Interstate 89

Interstate 89 in Vermont runs north to south for 130 miles from the United States/Canada border to the New Hampshire state line. Exit numbers are based on the consecutive numbering system. Northbound travelers should read up the chart. Southbound travelers read down the chart.

Exit(mm)	Description
14e	**US 2 / Williston Rd / Burlington**
	Pete's RV Center, 4015 Williston Rd, 802-864-9350, free. RV dealer is east of exit near the airport. Enter left of building. Dump station is at rear, complete drive around. Daylight hours only.
8	**Memorial Dr / Montpelier**
	Montpelier Municipal Sewage Plant on Dog River Rd, Free. From exit go east toward town; take first left on Dog River Rd; facility is on the left. Open during regular business hours. Ask at the office and they will unlock the gate. No water.

Interstate 91

Interstate 91 in Vermont runs north to south for 178 miles from the United States/Canada border to the Massachusetts state line. Exit numbers are based on the consecutive numbering system. Northbound travelers should read up the chart. Southbound travelers read down the chart.

Exit(mm)	Description
27	**VT 191 / Newport**
	Wastewater treatment plant in Newport. From exit go west about two miles to Western Ave and turn left; go 500 feet and turn right

onto TP Ln. Treatment plant can be seen from traffic light on left behind fire department.

1	US 5 / Brattleboro
	Fort Dummer State Park, 517 Old Guilford Rd, 802-254-2610, $10 fee

Other Locations

City or Town	Description
Jeffersonville	Madonna Mobil, 4828 VT Route 15, 802-644-5428, $9.99 plus tax. Latitude: 44.6477 • Longitude: -72.8295
Rutland	Wastewater treatment plant at West St (US 4 Bus) and Greens Hill Ln, free. 802-773-1863 Latitude: 43.6037 • Longitude: -72.9938
South Burlington	Water Pollution Control Dept., 1015 Airport Pkwy, 802-658-7964, free. Dump station is located at the wastewater treatment plant near the Burlington International Airport. Open daily 7am-3:30pm Mon-Fri. May be difficult for some to use because the dumping area is located at the end of the pavement and is also on the right side. There is no drive-through; you will have to back in to access dump. Latitude: 44.4815 • Longitude: -73.1703
White River Junction	Quechee State Park, 764 Dewey Mills Rd, White River Junction VT 05001 / 802-295-2990. Cost is $10. The state park is accessed from I-89 Exit 1 by following US 4 west about three miles. Open Memorial Day to October 15. Latitude: 43.6372 • Longitude: -72.4068

VIRGINIA

Below is a list of RV dump stations in Virginia. Listed first are those easily accessed from Interstate highways followed by those in other locations throughout the state.

Interstate 64

Interstate 64 runs east to west for 299 miles from I-264 in Chesapeake to the West Virginia state line. Part of it is shared with I-81. Eastbound travelers should read up the chart. Westbound travelers read down the chart.

Exit(mm)	Description
250b	**VA 105 / Fort Eustis Blvd / Newport News**
	Newport News Municipal Park campground at 13564 Jefferson Ave, 800-203-8322, $10 plus tax if not camping, free if camping. Latitude: 37.1874 • Longitude: -76.5581
	▼ *I-64 and I-81 run together / follows I-81 numbering* ▼
195	**US 11 / Lee Highway / near Lexington**
	Lee Hi Travel Plaza
	▲ *I-64 and I-81 run together / follows I-81 numbering* ▲

Interstate 77

Interstate 77 runs north to south for 67 miles from the West Virginia state line to the North Carolina state line. Part of it is also I-81. Northbound travelers should read up the chart. Southbound travelers read down the chart.

Exit(mm)	Description
41	**VA 610 / Peppers Ferry / Wytheville**
	TA Travel Center, 276-228-8676
	▼ *I-77 and I-81 run together / follows I-81 numbering* ▼
77	**Service Rd / near Wytheville**
	Flying J Travel Plaza
	▲ *I-77 and I-81 run together / follows I-81 numbering* ▲

Interstate 81

I-81 runs north to south for 325 miles from the West Virginia state line to the Tennessee state line. Portions are shared with I-64 and I-77. Northbound travelers should read up the chart. Southbound travelers read down the chart.

Exit(mm)	Description
323	**VA 669**
	Flying J Travel Plaza
	▼ *I-64 and I-81 run together / follows I-81 numbering* ▼
195	**US 11 / Lee Highway / near Lexington**
	Lee Hi Travel Plaza
	▲ *I-64 and I-81 run together / follows I-81 numbering* ▲
84	**VA 619 / to Grahams Forge**
	Love's Travel Stop
	▼ *I-77 and I-81 run together / follows I-81 numbering* ▼
77	**Service Rd / near Wytheville**
	Flying J Travel Plaza
	▲ *I-77 and I-81 run together / follows I-81 numbering* ▲
72	**I-77 N**
	TA Travel Center, 276-228-8676
	Comments: Use I-77 Exit 41
67	**US 11 (nb access only)**
	Wilco Travel Plaza

Interstate 85

Interstate 85 runs north to south for 69 miles from I-95 in Petersburg to the North Carolina state line. Northbound travelers should read up the chart. Southbound travelers read down the chart.

Exit(mm)	Description
39	**Old Stage Rd / near Warfield VA**
	Davis Travel Center, 12461 Old Stage Rd, Warfield VA 23889 / 804-478-4403. Free. Latitude: 36.9405 • Longitude: -77.7350

Interstate 95

Interstate 95 runs north to south for 179 miles from the Maryland state line to the North Carolina state line. Northbound travelers should read up the chart. Southbound travelers read down the chart.

Exit(mm)	Description
152	**VA 234 / Dumfries**
	Prince William Trailer Village, 2.5 miles west of exit on VA 234, $10. Clean facilities at the trailer park. Easy access, non-potable water hose available.
104	**VA 207 / to Bowling Green**
	Flying J Travel Plaza
98	**VA 30 / Doswell**
	Doswell All American Plaza
33	**SR-602 / Stony Creek**
	Davis Travel Center, 13306 St John Church Rd, Stony Creek VA 23882 / 434-246-2881. Free. Latitude: 36.9778 · Longitude: -77.3955
13	**Otterdam Rd / VA 614 / north of Emporia**
	Shell service station east of exit, no fee. Separate service islands for RVs. Has gas and diesel with dump station as part of service islands. Water is also available.
11b	**US 58 / W Atlantic St / Emporia**
	Sadler Travel Plaza, 918 W Atlantic St, Emporia VA 23847 / 434-634-4312. Free with fuel purchase, $10 without. Latitude: 36.7039 · Longitude: -77.5527
4	**Moores Ferry Rd / to Skippers**
	Love's Travel Stop, free

Other Locations

City or Town	Description
Amelia Court House	Amelia Family Campground, 9650 Military Rd, Amelia Court House VA 23002 / 804-561-3011. $10 fee if not camping. Campground is located .5 mile south of US-360 on SR-153. Metered LP gas available.
Bedford	Bedford Area Welcome Center off US 460 at the entrance to D-Day Memorial on Burks Hill Rd. Overnight RV parking is allowed ($10 per night); three sites have full hookups for $25 (one night stay only). Charge for use of the dump station is $5.

Centreville	Bull Run Regional Park off US 29, 703-631-0550, $21
Clarksville	Occoneechee State Park, 1192 Occoneechee Park Rd, 434-374-2210, $6.30. Upon entering park, proceed left and straight down the road following signs; dump is on the left. Latitude: 36.6355 • Longitude: -78.5290
Hampton	Gosnold's Hope Park (city park), 901 E Little Back River Rd, 757-850-5116. From I-64 Exit 263b, follow Mercury Blvd (US 278) east to King St. Follow King St north to Little Back River Rd and turn right (east). The park is approximately 3 miles on the left.
Reston	Lake Fairfax County Park campground off VA 606. You must be camping there to use it or pay the minimum overnight fee, which is about $8.
Montross	Westmoreland State Park, 804-493-8821, $3. Located six miles north of town via VA 3 and VA 347. Once in the park, look for sign to Campground B. Make a U-turn rather than going to Campground B. Dump station is ahead on right.
Salem	Tidy Services, 2011 Cook Dr, Salem VA 24153 / 540-345-0168. $20 disposal fee per RV/camper. Call-out pump service is also available. Open Mon-Fri, 7am-4pm; weekends, please call.
Virginia Beach	Dam Neck Navy Base (military ID required to gain access), no fee. Base has a small RV campground; dump is up the road from there. Water available and coin-op washing area to wash your RV.
Waynesboro	Sherando Lake Recreation Area (US Forest Service), $1 if not camping, free if camping. From I-64 take Exit 96 and follow VA 624 south to Lyndhurst and then VA 664 to campground. Recreation area is about ten miles off the interstate.

WASHINGTON

Below is a list of RV dump stations in Washington. Listed first are those easily accessed from Interstate highways followed by those in other locations throughout the state.

Interstate 5

I-5 runs north to south for 277 miles from the United States/Canada border to the Oregon state line. Northbound travelers should read up the chart. Southbound travelers read down the chart.

Exit(mm)	Description
258	**Bakerview Rd**
	Yorky's Exxon - free with fuel purchase, $4 without
256a	**WA 539 / Meridian St**
	Meridian Shell - dump station located behind car wash, limited to RVs up to 32 feet long
254	**Iowa St / State St**
	Iowa Street Chevron - free with fuel purchase, $3 without
232	**Cook Rd / Sedro-Woolley**
	Cook Road Texaco
231	**WA 11 / to Burlington**
	Camping World, 1240 Old Hwy 99, 866-337-4810, fee unknown
	Comments: There is a dump behind Foley's shop building. Appears to be for the convenience of Foley's shop operations; no signs. Poorly designed -- pavement is dead flat instead of being sloped toward the drain.
227	**College Way / Mount Vernon**
	Lions Park at 501 Freeway Dr
(207)	Rest Area
(188)	Rest Area (sb)
176	**N 175th St / Richmond Highlands**
	Evergreen RV Supply, 16610 Aurora Ave N, 206-542-1181, $3. Go west at exit and then south on Aurora Ave.
(141)	Rest Area (nb)
99	**WA 121 / 93rd Ave SW**
	Shell truck stop just west of exit, $10
48	**Huntington Ave / Castle Rock**
	Public dump station in Lion's Pride Park (city park), west of exit, donations requested. Clean water is also available.

(12)	Rest Area (sb)
(11)	Rest Area (nb)

Interstate 82

Interstate 82 runs east to west for 133 miles from the Oregon state line to I-90 exit 110 near Ellensburg. Eastbound travelers should read up the chart. Westbound travelers read down the chart.

Exit(mm)	Description
80	**Gap Rd**
	Rest Area
	Horse Heaven Hills Travel Plaza
54	**Yakima Valley Highway / Zillah**
	City-maintained dump station is on First Ave across from supermarket on west end of town, donation requested
52	**Meyers Rd / Zillah**
	City-maintained dump station is on First Ave across from supermarket on west end of town, donation requested
(24)	Rest Area (eb)
(22)	Rest Area (wb)

Interstate 90

Interstate 90 runs east to west for about 300 miles from the Idaho state line to I-5 in Seattle. Eastbound travelers should read up the chart. Westbound travelers read down the chart.

Exit(mm)	Description
289	**WA 27 / N Pines Rd / Opportunity**
	Divine's Shell gas station at N Pines Rd and E Mission Ave, west end of parking lot, $3.50. Latitude: 47.6710 • Longitude: -117.2395
287	**Mullan Rd / Argonne Rd / Milwood**
	Argonne & Montgomery Car Wash, 8805 E Montgomery Ave, Spokane WA 99212 / 509-924-3675. Free (donation). From exit, go N .3 mile on Mullan Rd/Argonne Rd then W .2 mile on Montgomery Ave. Open 24/7. Latitude: 47.6786 • Longitude: -117.2862
286	**E Broadway Ave / Spokane**
	Flying J Travel Plaza, 6606 E Broadway, 509-535-3028, free. Latitude: 47.6633 • Longitude: -117.3161

(242)	Rest Area (eb)
(199)	Rest Area (wb)
179	**WA 17**
	Husky Hillstop at 1253 Pioneer Way
	Moses Lake Exxon at 1725 Kittleson Rd
(162)	Rest Area (wb)
(161)	Rest Area (eb)
(89)	Rest Area
85	**Sunset Hwy / Cle Elum**
	Shell service station, free with fuel purchase
70	**Railroad St / Easton**
	Lake Easton State Park
17	**E Lake Sammamish Pkwy SE / Issaquah**
	Issaquah Village RV Park, 650 1st Ave NE, 800-258-9233, $5
15	**WA 900 / Renton Rd / Issaquah**
	Lake Sammamish State Park, $10 fee

Interstate 182

Interstate 182 runs east to west for about 14 miles from US 12 in Pasco to Interstate 82. Eastbound travelers should read up the chart. Westbound travelers read down the chart.

Exit(mm)	Description
5b	**George Washington Way / Richland**
	Columbia Point, no fee. From exit go north to first stop light and then east about one mile to city-owned boat launch.

Other Locations

City or Town	Description
Anacortes	Washington Park, 6300 Sunset Ave, Anacortes WA 98221 / 360-293-1927. City park is located about 4 miles west of town center via SR-20.
Anacortes	Wastewater treatment plant at 4th St and T Ave. From WA 20 follow R Ave to 4th St and turn right. No charge. Open weekdays 8:30am to 4:30 pm; 9am to 11am on holidays. Water fill station is nearby.
Bellevue	Shell Station at intersection of Richards Rd and SE 32nd St. Not easily reached from Freeways. Local map

	recommended. Washdown water at dump. Back in, with guidance. $3 with fill-up, $6 without.
Bremerton	Kitsap County Fairgrounds, 1200 NW Fairgrounds Rd, 360-337-5350, Free
Bremerton	Wastewater treatment plant near intersection of WA 3 and Loxie Eagans Blvd, free, take frontage road on southwest side of intersection behind Ford dealership, open 7am to 2pm Mon-Fri.
Buckley	Buckley Eagles Club, 29021 Hwy 410, Buckley WA 98321 / 360-829-1151. $5 donation. Latitude: 47.1586 • Longitude: -122.0423
Burlington	Lions Club Park at WA 20 and N Regent St, $1 donation requested, fresh water available at site
Burlington	Rotary Park on S Section St south of E Rio Vista Ave
Carson	A public dump station is located approximately 1.5 miles off Hwy 14 in the Columbia Gorge area. Take the Carson turnoff at Wind River Hwy. Go north about 100 yards past the WKO wood mill. Dump is located on the right side of the road. Fee is $2.
Chewelah	49er Motel & RV Park, 311 S Park St, $5 fee, south end of town on east side of US 395 (Park St)
Colfax	Palouse Empire Fairgrounds 5 miles west of Colfax on WA 26
Colville	Northeast Washington Fairgrounds on Astor Ave 3 blocks west of US 395
Colville	Whitty's Chevron at 370 W 5th Ave (US 395)
Connell	Scooteney Park Recreation Area (public) on Scooteney Reservoir about ten miles west of Connell via WA 260 and WA 17. Fee unknown
Coupeville	Waste treatment plant on NE 9th St. From SR-20 and N Main St, go north .5 mile to NE 9th St and turn east .3 mile. There is no water to rinse with. Free. Latitude: 48.2200 • Longitude: -122.6785
Dodge	Central Ferry Park about 12 miles north of town via WA 127; campground on Lake Bryan. Water available in summer. $5
Eatonville	Mill Town Shell, 360 Center St E, 360-832-6476, $5. Latitude: 46.8655 • Longitude: -122.2617
Elma	Gateway Exxon Truck Stop at US 12 Business and Main St
Elma	Rest area on WA 8 about two miles east of town. Free
Fairholm	Public campground in Olympic National Park at west end of Lake Crescent off US 101. $3 fee.

Friday Harbor	Wastewater treatment plant at intersection of Tucker Ave and Harbor St about 1/2 mile from ferry landing, no fee
Gold Bar	McDaniel's RV Park, 501 Croft Ave W, Gold Bar WA 98251 / 360-793-0181. $10. Latitude: 47.8588 • Longitude: -121.7039
Hatton	Hatton Coulee Rest Area at US 395 and WA 26 interchange; fee unknown
Hoodsport	Camp Cushman & Recreation Park, 7211 N Lake Cushman Rd, Hoodsport WA 98548 / 360-877-6770. $5 fee.
Hoodsport	Potlatch State Park on US-101 about 12 miles north of Shelton or 3 miles south of Hoodsport. Dump station fee is $5 if not camping.
Joyce	Salt Creek Recreation Area (county park) off WA 112 about 4 miles northeast of town
Kennewick	Columbia Park (city park), 1776 Columbia Park Trail, Free. Dump station is located next to the boat launch ramp near the marina.
Kennewick	Exxon gas station at 1st Ave and Washington, free with fill-up
Leavenworth	Lake Wenatchee State Park, $5 if not camping. The state park is located 18 miles north of Leavenworth, Washington, via US-2 and SR-207. The dump station is located in the North Campground. Latitude: 47.8123 • Longitude: -120.7209
Leavenworth	Nason Creek Rest Area along US 2 on north side of highway about three miles west of Coles Corner. Free
Lynden	Berthusen City Park at 8837 Berthusen Rd about three miles northwest of Lynden
Lynden	Cenex/Whatcom Farmers Co-op at corner of Main St and 3rd St, $2
Maple Falls	Silver Lake County Park - free to park guests, $5 for non-guests
Marysville	Public Works Dept at 1st St and Columbia Ave
Monroe	On US 2 (also WA 2) next to Sky Valley Traders store, $5 fee, pay inside store
Naches	RJ's Tire Factory, 10160 S Naches Road, Naches WA 98937 / 877-757 8473 or 509-653-2165. $5. Driving South on Highway 12 turn right into Naches Rd. Dump is 100 yards, at rear of Tire Factory.
Oak Harbor	Deception Pass State Park north of town, $5
Oak Harbor	Oak Harbor Beach Park (city park) near the junction of WA 20 and SE Pioneer Way. $3 fee.

Ocean Shores	A dump station is located next to the public works building on Point Brown Ave
Omak	Eastside Park on Omak Ave
Omak	Flying B, 600 Omache Dr, Omak WA 98841 / 509-826-4516. Fee not known. Latitude: 48.4167 • Longitude: -119.5097
Omak	Omak Chevron at 30 S Main St
Pasco	Chief's RV Center, 1120 N 28th Ave, Pasco WA 99301 / 800-345-1819 or 509-547-1198. Cost is $6. Latitude: 46.2380 • Longitude: -119.1279
Port Angeles	Clallam County Fair Grounds at 1608 W 16th St
Port Angeles	Road Runner Food Mart / 76 Station at 1023 E Front St
Port Orchard	Karcher Creek Wastewater Treatment Plant, Beach Dr and Olney Ave, 360-871-6861, no charge. Latitude: 47.6465 • Longitude: -122.6162
Port Orchard	Union 76 Station at WA 16 and Sedgwick Rd; located on the north side of the car wash; free
Pullman	City sewage plant on Park St, no fee, follow signs from WA 270
Raymond	Raymond RV & Marine, 1875 Ocean Ave, 360-942-2906, $5 fee. On US 101 about 1/2 mile west of town. Very easy to enter and exit. 12 RV sites on the Willapa River.
Republic	Slagle City Park at N Kean St and W 6th St (WA 20)
Sedro-Woolley	Wastewater treatment plant, 401 Alexander St, Free. From WA 20 at Township Rd, follow Township Rd south to Alexander St; turn right (west) to treatment plant.
Sequim	Chevron Station in town at east end of Washington St, next to Les Schwab Tires. $3 fee or free with fuel purchase.
Sequim	Dungeness Recreation Area (county park) on Lotzgesell Rd about 7 miles northwest of Sequim
Shelton	Mason County Fairgrounds at 751 W Fairgrounds Rd west of US 101, $10 fee
Spokane	Alderwood RV Resort, 14007 N Newport Way, Spokane WA 99021 / 888-847-0500 or 509-467-5320. Cost is $10. Latitude: 47.7853 • Longitude: -117.3537
Spokane	Riverside State Park, 509-465-5064. Dump station is located just inside campground gate near "Bowl and Pitcher" area on the Spokane River.
Stevenson	Heading east on SR-14, take the first left turn after the bridge coming into town (Sam's Autobody and Main Street Station). Follow the road around to the old grange

	on the left (about .5 mile). Public dump station is on the left side of the road, across from the apartments. Easy in and out for big rigs. $2 fee.
Stanwood	Camano Island State Park about 14 miles southwest of town. Free if you are camping, otherwise the fee is $5.
Sumas	Sumas RV Park & Campground, 9600 Easterbrook, 360-988-8875, $5
Tonasket	Visitor Center at 215 S Whitcomb - also has 8 RV camping sites with hookups
Walla Walla	Cenex Convenience Store at 706 W Rose St
Walla Walla	Lyons Park (city park) on Larch St at SE 12th St; in parking lot of park; donations accepted
Washougal	Public dump station at boat launch, west of town at WA Hwy 14 and South A St, $5
Wenatchee	Lincoln Rock State Park, 13253 US-2, East Wenatchee WA 98802 / 360-902-8844. Cost is $5 if not camping. The state park is about 8 miles north of town. Latitude: 47.5283 • Longitude: -120.2845
Wenatchee	Wenatchee Confluence State Park near US 2/97 and WA 285 junction in the Olds Station area, $5 fee.

WEST VIRGINIA

Below is a list of RV dump stations in West Virginia. Listed first are those easily accessed from Interstate highways followed by those in other locations throughout the state.

Interstate 64

Interstate 64 runs east to west for 189 miles from the Virginia state line to the Kentucky state line. Portions are shared with I-77 and the West Virginia Turnpike. Eastbound travelers should read up the chart. Westbound travelers read down the chart.

Exit(mm)	Description
▼	*I-64 and I-77 run together / follows I-77 numbering* ▼
45	**Vankirk Dr / Beckley**
	Beckley Travel Plaza/Tamarack Crafts Center
(72)	Turnpike Service Area (wb)
▲	*I-64 and I-77 run together / follows I-77 numbering* ▲
(35)	Rest Area

Interstate 68

I-68 is 32 miles long. It runs east to west from the Maryland state line to I-79 Exit 148 near Morgantown. Eastbound travelers should read up the chart. Westbound travelers read down the chart.

Exit(mm)	Description
(31)	Welcome Center (wb)

Interstate 70

Interstate 70 runs east to west for 14 miles from the Pennsylvania state line to the Ohio state line. Eastbound travelers should read up the chart. Westbound travelers read down the chart.

Exit(mm)	Description
(13)	Welcome Center (wb) - dump station is closed in winter

11	**WV 41 / Dallas Pike**
	Dallas Pike Travel Express

Interstate 77

I-77 runs north to south for 187 miles from the Ohio state line to the Virginia state line. Portions are also I-64 and the West Virginia Turnpike. Northbound travelers should read up the chart. Southbound travelers read down the chart.

Exit(mm)	Description
185	Welcome Center, 1325 Highland Ave, Williamstown WV 26187 / 304-375-2700. Free. Dump station open May-Sep
(166)	Rest Area (nb). Free. Dump station open May-Sep
	▼ *I-64 and I-77 run together / follows I-77 numbering* ▼
(72)	Turnpike Service Area (nb)
45	**Vankirk Dr / Beckley**
	Beckley Travel Plaza/Tamarack Crafts Center
	▲ *I-64 and I-77 run together / follows I-77 numbering* ▲
(17)	Turnpike Service Area (nb)

Interstate 79

Interstate 79 runs north to south for 161 miles from the Pennsylvania state line to I-77 exit 104 near Charleston. Northbound travelers should read up the chart. Southbound travelers read down the chart.

Exit(mm)	Description
(159)	Welcome Center (sb)
(123)	Rest Area
(85)	Rest Area
(49)	Rest Area

Other Locations

City or Town	Description
Harpers Ferry	KOA, 343 Campground Rd, 304-535-6895, $5. Located near Harpers Ferry National Historical Park off US 340.
New Martinsville	Public dump station on the corner of Main St and Harlan Dr near the public park/boat launch, no fee

WISCONSIN

Below is a list of RV dump stations in Wisconsin. Listed first are those easily accessed from Interstate highways followed by those in other locations throughout the state.

Interstate 39

Interstate 39 is about 205 miles long. It runs north to south from US 51 in Merrill to the Illinois state line. Part of it is also shared with I-90 and I-94. Northbound travelers should read up the chart. Southbound travelers read down the chart.

Exit(mm)	Description
192	**WI 29 / WI 52 / Stewart Ave / Wausau**
	Marathon Park (county), 715-261-1550, 35-site campground with electricity, dump station at west end of park, fee unknown.
188	**Rib Mountain Dr / CR N / to Wausau**
	Rib Mountain Travel Center
	▼ I-39, I-90 & I-94 run together / follows I-90 numbering ▼
126	**CR V / De Forest**
	Madison KOA, 4859 County Road V, De Forest WI 53532 / 608-846-4528. Cost is $7. Open April 1st to November 1st. Latitude: 43.2488 • Longitude: -89.3702
132	**US 51 / to Madison**
	Token Creek Park (county park), $6 fee
	Wisconsin RV World
	▲ I-39, I-90 & I-94 run together / follows I-90 numbering ▲

Interstate 43

Interstate 43 runs north to south for 192 miles from US 41 in Green Bay to I-90/I-39 in Beloit. Portions of it is shared with I-94 and I-894. Northbound travelers should read up the chart. Southbound travelers read down the chart.

Exit(mm)	Description
187	**East Shore Dr / N Webster Ave / Green Bay**
	Bay Beach City Park

157	**CR V / Hillcrest Rd / Francis Creek**
	Fun-N-Fast Travel Center

Interstate 90

Interstate 90 runs east to west for 188 miles from the Illinois state line to the Minnesota state line. Parts of it are shared with I-39 and I-94. Eastbound travelers should read up the chart. Westbound travelers read down the chart.

Exit(mm)	Description
▼ *I-39, I-90 & I-94 run together / follows I-90 numbering* ▼	
132	**US 51 / to Madison**
	Token Creek Park (county park), $6 fee
	Wisconsin RV World
126	**CR V / De Forest**
	Madison KOA, 4859 County Road V, De Forest WI 53532 / 608-846-4528. Cost is $7. Open April 1st to November 1st. Latitude: 43.2488 • Longitude: -89.3702
▲ *I-39, I-90 & I-94 run together / follows I-90 numbering* ▲	
▼ *I-90 & I-94 run together / follows I-90 numbering* ▼	
69	**WI 82 / Mauston**
	Kwik Trip
61	**WI 80 / New Lisbon**
	New Lisbon Travel Center
	Bunkhouse Travel Center, 1700 E Bridge St, New Lisbon WI 53950 / 608-562-6000. $10 fee.
▲ *I-90 & I-94 run together / follows I-90 numbering* ▲	

Interstate 94

I-94 runs east to west for about 350 miles from the Illinois state line to the Minnesota state line. Portions are shared with I-39, I-43, and I-90. Eastbound travelers should read up the chart. Westbound travelers read down the chart.

Exit(mm)	Description
333	**WI-20 / Washington Ave / Sturtevant**
	Burlington RV Superstore, 390 S Sylvania Ave, Sturtevant WI 53177 / 888-783-2645 or 262-321-2500. Free. Open 24 hours a day, 7 days a week.

322	**WI 100 / W Ryan Rd / to Oak Creek**
	Flying J Travel Plaza

319	**W College Ave / Milwaukee**
	Prosser RV / Cruise America, 6146 S Howell Ave, 414-766-1079, $35 fee. Full-service dump (no do-it-yourself) by appointment only. From exit, go east to WI 38 (Howell Ave) and turn left (north); one block on east side of street.

306	**WI 181 / S 84th St / Milwaukee**
	Wisconsin State Fair Park south of exit. Dump station is beside campground and has plenty of turnaround space. $8

▼ *I-39, I-90 & I-94 run together / follows I-90 numbering* ▼

132	**US 51 / to Madison**
	Token Creek Park (county park), $6 fee
	Wisconsin RV World

126	**CR V / De Forest**
	Madison KOA, 4859 County Road V, De Forest WI 53532 / 608-846-4528. Cost is $7. Open April 1st to November 1st. Latitude: 43.2488 • Longitude: -89.3702

▲ *I-39, I-90 & I-94 run together / follows I-90 numbering* ▲
▼ *I-90 & I-94 run together / follows I-90 numbering* ▼

69	**WI 82 / Mauston**
	Kwik Trip

61	**WI 80 / New Lisbon**
	New Lisbon Travel Center
	Bunkhouse Travel Center, 1700 E Bridge St, New Lisbon WI 53950 / 608-562-6000. $10 fee.

▲ *I-90 & I-94 run together / follows I-90 numbering* ▲

143	**US 12 / WI 21 / Tomah**
	Kwik Trip, dump is located behind main building next to small out building.

116	**WI 54 / Black River Falls**
	Black River Crossing Oasis
	Flying J Travel Plaza, 715-284-4341, Latitude: 44.2952 • Longitude: -90.8302

65	**MN 37 / MN 85 / Eau Claire**
	Eau Claire wastewater treatment plant on Ferry St. From exit go north to Short St and turn left. Go to stop sign (Ferry St) and turn left. Follow to the end of the road, through treatment plant gates, and follow signs. Open 7am to 10pm all week. Free

Other Locations

City or Town	Description
Abbotsford	Shell Travel Center on west side of town off WI 29, no fee. Huge lot with lots of space for pulling and turning around.
Antigo	Antigo Lake RV Park in downtown Antigo; east of US 45; rinse water available.
Antigo	Wastewater treatment plant, N2420 Koszarek Rd, 715-623-2797, $5. From US 45 south of town, go west 1/2 mile on County Road X to Koszarek Rd, go south to plant. Latitude: 45.1141 • Longitude: -89.1641
Ashland	Kreher Park (city park) in Ashland, three blocks north of US 2 at Prentice Ave N, no charge. Latitude: 46.5955 • Longitude: -90.8817
Baileys Harbor	Baileys Grove Travel Park and Campground, 2552 CR F, $10
Baraboo	BP station on WI 33 about three miles east of US 12, $5
Baraboo	Devil's Lake State Park, free but a daily or seasonal park sticker is required for entrance to park. From US 12 travel east on Hwy 159 1/2 mile to Hwy 123. Turn right and follow to main entrance to park. Follow curve in road to left before entering park and proceed down the hill. Turn onto first road to the right, which is actually an entrance to one of the campground, and follow circle all the way around going right. Dump station will be on your right side when you have almost completely circled back to the entrance you came in at.
Baraboo	Wastewater treatment plant off WI 113, free. Go south from Circus World museum to Manchester St and turn right. Plant is 1/4 mile on your left.
Beaver Dam	Derge County Park about 7 miles northwest of town via County Road G and County Road CP. Cost is $7.
Boulder Junction	North Trout Lake Campground (Northern Highland State Forest), no fee. Campground is about six miles off US 51 via CR M or three miles south of town. Turn left at campground and then first right and follow to dump station.
Cadott	River Country Plaza at WI 27 and WI 29
Cassville	Riverside Park at Wall St and Prime St. Dump is located at south end of park near the boat ramp between rest rooms and railroad track. Free

Chippewa Falls	Wastewater treatment plant, 1125 W River St (WI 29), 715-726-2745, free, across from River Country Co-op
Colby	Super 29 Shell at 1210 WI 13
Columbus	Astico County Park at WI 16/60 and CR TT about 3 miles east of Columbus
De Pere	Brown County Fairgrounds, 1500 Fort Howard Ave, 920-336-7292, $5, west side of Fox River. Latitude: 44.4605 • Longitude: -88.0722
Eagle River	Wastewater treatment plant on W Division St, west of US 45, $5 fee. Very large area to turn around. Rinse water available. Open 24/7
Elkhart Lake	Broughton Sheboygan Marsh Park (county park) about two miles northwest of town, $10 fee
Ellsworth	Public dump station in the Pierce County Fairgrounds on the north end of Ellsworth along SR-65. Camping with electric hookups also available.
Fond du Lac	County fairgrounds at E 17th St and Martin Ave, no fee. The dump that was for non-campers was removed; you must back into a site and dump at a site.
Granton	Beckers BP Highway Service on US 10 between Marshfield and Neillsville, no fee. Sells diesel as well as gas. Also has a convenience store.
Green Bay	Van Boxtel RV Center at 1956 Bond St, no fee. From US 41, take the WI 29/Shawano Ave exit, east to N Taylor St, north to Bond St. Open Mon-Fri, 9am-6pm; Sat, 9am-5pm. Latitude: 44.5416 • Longitude: -88.0700
Hilbert	Calumet County Park, 10 miles west of town via WI 114, WI 55 and CR EE, $3. Latitude: 44.1017 • Longitude: -88.3219
Jefferson	Jefferson County Fair Park, 503 N Jackson Ave, 920-674-7148, $5. Dump station is at the south end of the complex.
Junction City	DuBay Park (county park), 31-site campground about nine miles northeast of town via US 10, WI 34, and CR E. $5 or free if camping.
Kieler	Rustic Barn Campground, 3854 Dry Hollow Rd, 608-568-7797, $5 charge, open mid-April to mid-October. Located west of US 61/151 about 8 miles northeast of Dubuque, Iowa.
Marshfield	Central Wisconsin State Fairgrounds at S Vine Ave and E 17th St
McFarland	Babcock Park (county park) on Lake Waubesa along US 51, $5. Campground has 25 sites with electric hookups.

Merrill	Council Grounds State Park, 715-536-8773, $3 fee plus park entrance fee. Park is west of town via WI 107.
Middleton	Mendota Park (county park), 5130 Cty Hwy M, Middleton WI 53562 / 608-246-3896. Cost is $5 for non-campers. Park is located east of town off County Highway M near the intersection of County Highways Q and M. On the west side of Lake Mendota. Latitude: 43.1118 • Longitude: -89.4691
Minocqua	Lakeland Sanitary District at 8780 Morgan Rd about 2 1/2 miles northwest of town via US 51 and WI 70
Minong	Link Stop convenience store and A&W on US 53 behind the store by the LP tank. Open year-round, $5, rinse water available, no rinse hose.
Mosinee	Big Eau Pleine Park (county park), 106-site campground about 12 miles southwest of town via WI 153 and Eau Pleine Park Rd. Fee unknown.
New Franken	Bay Shore Park (county park), 5637 Sturgeon Bay Rd, New Franken WI 54229 / 920-448-4466 (Parks Department). $5 fee if not camping. Park is just off of SR-57 about 15 miles northeast of Green Bay. Latitude: 44.6352 • Longitude: -87.8030
New Richmond	Hatfield Park (city park) off SR-64 at Knowles Ave. Phone: 715-243-0440. Cost is $5. Latitude: 45.1362 • Longitude: -92.5342
Oconto	Holtwood Park (city park) west of US 41, $2. Turn west at the south end of Oconto River Bridge and go about four blocks; turn right to campground; dump on right side of road.
Oshkosh	BP-Oshkosh Plaza on Green Valley Rd at US 41 and WI 76, $5 fee, 920-233-1165
Park Falls	City of Park Falls Public Works Department on Case Ave about 1/4 mile south of WI 182. Free.
Platteville	City Garage on Valley Road off US 151
Reedsburg	BP/Amoco at WI 33 and CR H, no fee
Rhinelander	Wastewater treatment plant on Boyce Dr about 1/4 mile south of Kemp St; free for residents, $3 for others
Rice Lake	Cenex service station of US 53 Exit 143, 715-736-0800. Free. Dump station is in back of the store.
Richland Center	City wastewater treatment plant on S Orange St west of US 14, no fee. Dump station accessible from US 14 between intersections of Seminary St and southbound WI 80. City posted a small red "RV Dump Station" sign. Limited turnaround for big rigs or rigs towing vehicles.

River Falls	Hoffman Park one block west of WI 35 off Division St (CR M), $2
Sauk City	Cenex station at 740 Phillips Blvd (US 12), $3 fee, free with fill-up.
Shawano	Shawano County Fairgrounds at 990 E Green Bay St in town
Shawano	Shawano County Park at W5785 Lake Dr, about 5 miles northeast of town via WI 47 and CR H
Siren	Holiday gas station, 24096 State Road 35 (2nd Ave), 715-349-2410, fee unknown
Slinger	Campground in the Pike Lake Unit of Kettle Moraine State Forest, $4. Park is located along WI 60 between Slinger and Hartford.
Stevens Point	Jordan Park (county park), 1903 County Hwy Y, 715-346-1433, $5. The park can be accessed from I-39 Exit 159 by following WI 66 north three miles and then CR Y to park entrance. Latitude: 44.5781 • Longitude: -89.5012
Stoughton	Lake Kegonsa State Park, 2405 Door Creek Rd, 608-873-9695, potable water available. The dump station is open during camping season (May-Oct). Latitude: 42.9773 • Longitude: -89.2324
Superior	BP gas station southeast end of town on the northeast side of US 2. Easy access. Free with gas purchase, $5 without. They also have potable and non-potable water available.
Tomah	Public dump station at Fort McCoy on WI 21. The dump is free to the public but you will need to show a picture ID when going through the gate.
Tomahawk	Public dump station behind city garage on US 51 Bus, three blocks west of Higly's Propane & Appliance store in downtown Tomahawk, no fee.
Washburn	Memorial Park (city park) off WI 13 at 6th Ave E, north end of town. Fee unkown.
Webster	Public dump station in Lions Park west of SR-35 on Apple St at Musky St (south end of town). Free. Water is available.
Wisconsin Rapids	City wastewater treatment plant at 2540 1st St S (east of Riverview Expy Bridge), $1 fee, non-potable water for flushing tanks available as is potable water for freshwater tank

WYOMING

Below is a list of RV dump stations in Wyoming. Listed first are those easily accessed from Interstate highways followed by those in other locations throughout the state.

Interstate 25

Interstate 25 runs north to south for 300 miles from I-90 in Buffalo to the Colorado state line. Northbound travelers should read up the chart. Southbound travelers read down the chart.

Exit(mm)	Description
299	**US 16 / Buffalo**
	Big Horn Travel Plaza, 207 S Bypass Rd, 307-684-5246, $3 fee
	Cenex Truck Stop, 501 E Hart St, 307-684-9513, free
185	**WY 258 / Wyoming Blvd / Casper**
	Flying J Travel Plaza, 41 SE Wyoming Blvd, 307-473-1750
182	**WY 253 / Brooks Rd / Hat Six Rd**
	Eastgate Travel Plaza
140	**W Yellowstone Hwy / Douglas**
	North Platte River City Park, Douglas WY 82633 / 307-358-3462. Free. Latitude: 42.7624 • Longitude: -105.3918
126	**US 18 / US 20 / Orin**
	Rest Area
	Orin Junction Truck Stop
92	**US 26 / north of Wheatland**
	Rest Area, dump station is located in the northwest corner
78	**Mariposa Pkwy / Wheatland**
	Lewis Park (city park), 600 9th St, Wheatland WY 82201 / 307-322-2962. Free. From exit go E 1 block, S 1 block on 16th St, E .5 mile on Cole (watch for a bad dip in the road along Cole), N on 8th St to park. Latitude: 42.0476 • Longitude: -104.9539
(54)	Rest Area
12	**Central Ave / Cheyenne**
	Public dump station at Lake Absarraca northwest of Carey Ave at Kennedy Rd. From the exit, go east to Kennedy Rd and turn right. Dump station is on dirt road just north of the end of Carey Ave. No water for rinsing tanks. Free. Latitude: 41.1603 • Longitude: -104.8346

7 **WY 212 / College Dr**
Welcome Center, Cheyenne WY 82007 / 307-777-7777. Free.
Northwest corner of exit, north of McDonalds. Two dump stations,
spacious parking for big rigs. Open year-round but flush water is
shut off during cold season.

Flying J Travel Plaza, 2250 Etchepare Dr, 307-635-2918. Free.
Latitude: 41.0986 • Longitude: -104.8536
Comments: It is in a tight location that limits its usefulness
when the truck stop is busy, which is often.

Love's Travel Stop, 3305 W College Dr, 307-632-2444, free

Interstate 80

Interstate 80 runs east to west for about 403 miles from the Nebraska
state line to the Utah state line. Eastbound travelers should read up the
chart. Westbound travelers read down the chart.

Exit(mm)	Description
370	**US 30 / Archer**
	Sapp Brothers Truck Stop, 3350 I-80 Service Rd, 307-632-6600, $5 fee
311	**WY 130 / WY 230 / Snowy Range Rd / Laramie**
	High Country Sportsman
	Wyoming Territorial Prison, 975 Snowy Range Rd, Laramie WY 82070 / 307-745-6161. $5 Latitude: 41.3109 • Longitude: -105.6104
214	**Higley Blvd / Rawlins**
	Rip Griffin Travel Center
209	**Johnson Rd**
	Flying J Travel Plaza
173	**Wamsutter**
	Love's Travel Stop, 314 Kelly Rd, 307-324-0087
	Sinclair Fuel Stop
	Wamsutter Conoco Service
104	**US 191 / Elk St / Rock Springs**
	Flying J Travel Plaza, 650 Stagecoach Dr, 307-362-4231, free
68	**Little America**
	Little America Truck Stop
6	**I-80 Bus / Bear River Dr / Evanston**
	Bear River Travel Information Center, 601 Bear River Dr, 307-789-6540, $5

Interstate 90

Interstate 90 runs east to west for 208 miles from the South Dakota state line to the Montana state line. Eastbound travelers should read up the chart. Westbound travelers read down the chart.

Exit(mm)	Description
126	**WY 59 / Gillette**
	Dalbey Memorial Park one mile south of exit off WY 59
	Flying J Travel Plaza, 1810 Douglas Hwy, 307-682-3562, free
25	**US 14 / WY 334 / Sheridan**
	Holiday Gas Station, south of exit, 936 E Brundage Ln, 307-672-8729, free
	Comments: Dump station is located on the southwest corner of the gas station and is best accessed by smaller RVs. May be closed in winter.
	Washington City Park, on Coffeen Ave
	Comments: From I-90 exit proceed west to first traffic light and turn right. Proceed about one mile and cross Little Goose Creek bridge. Park is about 1/4 mile beyond the bridge on the right.
23	**WY 330 / 5th St / Sheridan**
	Visitor Information Center, closed in winter

Other Locations

City or Town	Description
Afton	City of Afton information center, free
Alpine	Nordic Market at US 89 and US 26
Baggs	City Hall maintains a free dump station with potable water. Check in at City Hall. Very easy access right off SH-789, center of town.
Basin	Overland Express Mart, 155 N 4th St, 307-568-2722, free
Basin	Washington Park (city park), open May thru Sep, 307-568-3331, free
Buffalo	Bighorn National Forest public dump station on US 16 about three miles west of Powder River Pass, on south side of highway, fresh water available, donation

Burgess Junction	Bighorn National Forest public dump station 1/4 mile east of US 14/14A junction, north side of road, donation requested, fresh water available
Casper	Bentz's Town Pump, 701 W Collins Dr, 307-234-1435, $2.50 fee for standard RVs. Also offers a portable dump catch basin for buses, $10 fee.
Casper	Rest Area on WY 220 adjacent to Independence Rock on the Oregon Trail about 53 miles southwest of Casper
Cody	City of Cody dump station located 1/2 mile east of Cody, next to the Wyoming Vietnam Memorial Park, on the north side of highway. Donations accepted.
Cokeville	Flying J Travel Plaza at US 30 and WY 232
Green River	Wastewater treatment plant on E Astle Ave, free
Guernsey	Guernsey State Park, 307-836-2334. Guernsey State Park is located off Interstate 25, Exit 92 to U.S. Highway 26 and then State Route 270. A dump station is located at the south entrance to Guernsey State Park.
Jackson	Reynolds Petroleum, 1055 W Broadway, free with fill-up, without fill-up a fee of $5 to $25 is charged depending on size of RV
Jackson	Wrangler Petroleum, 580 W Broadway, also has propane, dump available in summer only
Lander	Popo Agie One Stop at 8116 E Main St (US 287)
Lander	Public Works Dept., 125 Buena Vista Dr, 307-332-3956, Free. Latitude: 42.8297 • Longitude: -108.7248
Lovell	City park at E 2nd St and Quebec Ave
Pinedale	Warren Bridge Campground (Bureau of Land Management) about 20 miles northwest of town via US 191. $3
Riverton	Bob's Hilltop Sinclair, 912 W Main St, 307-856-1412, $2 fee
Riverton	C-Plus Conoco, 203 N Federal Blvd (US 26), 307-856-1100
Riverton	Wind River RV Park, 1618 E Park Ave, 800-528-3913, $10. RV Park is 6 blocks east of US 26.
Shoshoni	Trail Town Supply at US 20 and US 26
Sinclair	Seminoe State Park, Box 30 HCR 67, Sinclair WY 82334 / 307-320-3013. The dump station is located in the North Red Hills camping area.
Thermopolis	Texaco Southside Travel Center at 167 US 20
Torrington	Torrington Travel Terminal at 1500 US 26
Wright	Rest area on WY 387, just west of WY 59

APPENDIX A

How to Empty Holding Tanks

Here's a suggestion on how to empty your RV's holding tanks.

First of all, don't open any valves until the proper time! Doing so will be met with rather unpleasant results. You may consider wearing a pair of rubber gloves in the event some effluent gets on your hands. Some folks will also wear rubber boots. As long as you're careful, any splashing is minimal.

Remove the holding tank outlet cap and connect your three-inch sewer hose to the outlet of your holding tank. Extend the hose to the opening of the dump station, which is usually a hole in the ground that is slightly larger than the three-inch hose.

Insert your sewer hose into the dump station's hole about four to six inches. Use the hole's cover, a brick, or something heavy enough to hold the sewer hose in place so it doesn't come out of the hole.

Once you're sure that all is connected and held down, open your black tank valve. You'll hear the effluent flow and eventually it'll slow, then stop. Close the black tank valve.

Now open the gray tank valve. Again, you'll hear water flow, then slow, and stop. Close the gray tank valve.

At this point, you're almost done. If you want to flush and rinse your tanks once more, you can do so by filling your tanks to two-thirds full and repeat the emptying process. If others are waiting to use the dump station, skip this step.

Recheck that both your black and gray water tank valves are closed and disconnect the sewer hose from your tank outlet. Replace the tank outlet cover. Lift the end of the sewer hose (the end you just disconnected) to completely drain the hose into the dump station. If a non-potable water hose is available, run water through the sewer hose to rinse it out. Remove the sewer hose from the dump station hole and rinse the outside of the hose. Rinse the area around the hole to ensure that any spillage has been cleaned up and cover the dump station hole.

Go in to your RV and add about five gallons of water (about three flushes) to your black tank and then add the appropriate amount of holding tank treatment. If you use a treatment for your gray tank, do that as well.

The task of emptying your RV's holding tanks is finished! Now it's time to move on to your next destination.

APPENDIX B

Dump Station Tips

Here are some tips to follow when emptying your RV's holding tanks.

- Don't dump the black-water tank until it is at least two-thirds full. Don't leave the black-water tank valve open when hooked up at a campsite. This will cause liquids to drain, leaving solid waste behind to harden on the bottom of the tank.

- Use a heavy-duty sewer hose about 6 to 8 feet long to make handling easier.

- Carry an extra garden hose for rinsing in case the dump station doesn't have one. Store this in an area where it won't come into contact with your drinking water hose.

- Never use your fresh water hose for rinsing sewer hoses or the dump station area.

- Wear protective rubber gloves and avoid touching the outside of the gloves.

- If others are waiting to use the dump station, skip the tank flushing and hose rinsing steps. Pull away from the dump station and then add some water and chemicals to the holding tanks.

- Never put anything other than the contents of your holding tanks into the dump station.

- Leave the dump station area cleaner than you found it.

APPENDIX C

Dump Station Abuse

For years RVers have been pulling into Interstate rest areas and other areas with free dump stations to empty their holding tanks. But because of abuse, many states are removing dump stations from their rest areas and campground owners and others view their dump stations as an expensive maintenance headache. Dump station abuse amounts to folks leaving a mess or putting things into the dump drain that just don't belong there. Remember, somebody has to clean up the mess or clean out the drain. Dump station abuse causes aggravation, creates a health hazard, and costs money. You can do your part to ensure RVers will continue to have free and clean dump stations by following the simple tips mentioned in Appendix B.